NEVER
GIVE UP

NEVER GIVE UP

MY STROKE, MY RECOVERY, AND MY RETURN TO THE NFL

TEDY BRUSCHI

with Michael Holley

WILEY

John Wiley & Sons, Inc.

Published by John Wiley & Sons, Inc., Hoboken, New Jersey
Published simultaneously in Canada

Color insert photo credits: page 12, *Boston Herald*; all others, David Silverman/New England Patriots

Design and composition by Navta Associates, Inc.

For general information about our other products and services, please contact our Customer Care Department within the United States at (800) 762-2974, outside the United States at (317) 572-3993 or fax (317) 572-4002.

Wiley also publishes its books in a variety of electronic formats. Some content that appears in print may not be available in electronic books. For more information about Wiley products, visit our web site at www.wiley.com.

Library of Congress Cataloging-in-Publication Data:

Bruschi, Tedy.
    Never give up : my stroke, my recovery, and my return to the NFL / Tedy Bruschi with Michael Holley.
    ISBN 978-0-470-10869-7 (cloth)
    ISBN 978-0-470-37354-5 (paper)
1. Bruschi, Tedy. 2. Football players—United States—Biography. 3. Cerebrovascular disease—Patients—United States—Biography. 4. New England Patriots (Football team) I. Holley, Michael, 1970- II. Title.
    GV939.B7847A3 2007
    796.332092—dc22
    [B]

                                                                20070080507

Printed in the United States of America
10 9 8 7 6 5 4 3 2

For our sons, TJ, Rex, and Dante. With faith, courage, and love, all is possible. We love you.

Contents

CONTENTS

Foreword

by Tom Brady

When I arrived at my first training camp, I learned quickly that Coach Belichick never accepts excuses and always expects his players to have the toughness and determination to pay an individual price for the team's success. The players who fit this mold formed the core of our 2001 championship team. Those who didn't found work elsewhere.

That's why as a first-year player I emulated Tedy Bruschi. I would stay a step behind him walking to practice and sit a few rows behind him in meetings and on bus rides, watching how he carried himself in his interactions with everyone from the ball boys to Mr. Kraft. He doesn't have to give locker room speeches; Tedy lets his actions speak for themselves. His ferocity on the field, his determination on every play, and his willingness to do whatever it takes to win is what separates him from the competition. He is the rock on which our championship franchise has been built, because he is what being a New England Patriot is all about.

I believe our Super Bowl XXXIX championship capped Tedy's finest season, and he received a long-overdue selection to the Pro Bowl. I was fortunate to be chosen as well, so we got to hang out like never before. We jet-skied, toured Pearl Harbor, visited U.S. naval facilities, and shared plenty of laughs. We played in the Pro Bowl and that night found ourselves in the hotel lobby reflecting on how lucky we were to experience winning a third Super Bowl. We talked about our families and the support they had for us. We talked about our off-season plans and what it was going to take to get back to the big game. We then grabbed a bus together to the airport, Tedy flying back to Boston and me to Mexico for some relaxation.

Less than forty-eight hours later I returned to my hotel room and logged on to my computer to find that Tedy had been rushed to Massachusetts General Hospital after suffering what we later found out was a stroke. "How could this happen?" I wondered. He had just walked away from me in the airport as strong of mind, body, and soul as any man I knew, and now this.

Following the stroke there was nationwide speculation on whether Tedy would be able to recover. Most thought football was out of the question. The outpouring of support from Tedy's fans and friends was incredible. I never had a doubt that Tedy would be ready to play football again at some point following his stroke. I knew he could overcome anything, even something as difficult as a potentially career-ending injury. I sat in his house a few weeks after his surgery looking at the huge bruises all over his body, Tedy still without full vision, still exhausted from the surgery, and yet I saw the same fire in his eyes that had been inspiring me for years. This life-altering experience had taken all of his energy from him and hurt him badly, but I knew it hadn't taken his toughness and determination.

Tedy gives you something to believe in. Whether we're winning or losing, he holds his head high, and he knows himself and handles himself so well, others can't help but follow him. The way he practices and plays forces you to become a better teammate; the way he demands hustle and toughness forces you to become a better leader; and the way he carries himself inspires you to become a better person. This made his return to playing on October 30 against Buffalo all the more electrifying. The stadium was louder that night than on the nights we had raised our Super Bowl banners. Our captain, our leader, our inspiration was back on the field doing what he loved to do. Tedy had spent months rehabbing, had countless doctor visits, and had undergone hundreds of tests trying to play again. Just *eight* months after our victory in Super Bowl XXXIX, here we were celebrating a much bigger victory on our home field. Sure it was great to win the game, but that night we were celebrating Tedy's return as he showed us teammates, fans, family, and friends what it takes to become victorious in life.

What you get from Tedy on the field, however, is just a glimpse of all that he is. He is witty but reserved, patient but fiery, determined but elusive. Tedy has all the qualities you look for in a best friend, a father, and a role model, all in one person. It's rare to come across a man who has his feet firmly planted on the ground and who never sacrifices what is true and honest to him.

I was excited to participate in this book because I'm excited for the fans of the Patriots to get to know the man like I know him. Over the past eight years I have been lucky for many reasons, not the least of which has been my friendship with "Bru."

We've developed a brotherly bond through countless practices, meals, victory parties, and family events. I am proud of who he is and what he has overcome, and I look forward to many more years of growth together and, of course, winning a few more championships.

You might be coming to this book as a fan of Tedy's football skills and, don't get me wrong, gaining the insights of one of the best defenders in Patriots history is worth the price of admission, but that's just part of the story. There are a lot of reasons to look up to him, and I promise you will finish this book with an admiration for him on a much deeper level.

Preface

I never really felt like I had much to say, but after my stroke that changed. I've received countless letters from so many people: football fans and stroke survivors—many of whom have been in life struggles that they feel can't be overcome. They all ask me, "How did you do it?" I want to respond to every letter and e-mail, but it's just not possible. This book is my answer to all of those people. I feel it's a story that should be told because I want people to know that life is special, and you should enjoy all the good it has to offer, but you are truly defined by how you respond to the struggles it presents to you.

I look forward to using this book to educate people on the warning signs of stroke. To show our commitment, Michael and I are going to donate a portion of our proceeds to the American Stroke Association.

> Tedy Bruschi
> Linebacker
> Stroke Survivor

Acknowledgments

This journey would not have been possible without the help of so many special people. My wife, Heidi, who gave me courage when I had none left. My entire family, who gave me strength and support. Tony and Linda, when I needed you most you were right there. Vicki and Kati, you were everything for us. Bill and Sharon Roberts, Tracie Pond, and Sue Bowen. Friends always say, "Call if you need anything." Thanks for answering our call.

To all of the doctors, nurses, and staff at Massachusetts General Hospital, thank you for being so kind. Dr. Greer, your professionalism, expertise, and humor helped me more than you could possibly know. Dr. Igor Palacios, Mary Lievens, Dr. Danita Sanborn, and Dr. Era Demergian, I know at times I was not the best patient; thank you for your kindness. Karen and the gang, you made things so easy for Heidi and me. Also, Anne McCarthy Jacobson and the people at Spaulding Rehabilitation Hospital, thanks for being so tough on me. Anne, I needed that. I would also like to express my sincere gratitude to Dr. Art Day of Brigham and Women's hospital in Boston and Dr. Matthew

Fink and Dr. Gatto at the New York–Presbyterian Hospital/ Weill Cornell Medical Center.

The support of the New England Patriots organization was incredible. One of my earliest memories at the hospital was seeing a blurry Robert and Myra Kraft at my bedside. Thank you both so much for your support and compassion. To my coaches and teammates past and present, you all were instrumental in helping me return to the field. Tom Brady, Mike Vrabel, Rosevelt Colvin, Larry Izzo, Willie McGinest, Roman Phifer, and all the 'backers; Rodney Harrison; Christian Fauria; Richard Seymour; Dan Koppen; Deion Branch; Adam Vinatieri; Jarvis Green; Rodney Bailey; and Joe Andruzzi, I could name you all and you all will forever be "my boys." My head coach, Bill Belichick, thanks for seeing things clearly when I could not and having faith that I could complete this comeback. Thanks to Scott Pioli for your support and trust. A special thanks to our training staff, Jim Whalen, Joe Van Allen, and Dave Granito. From staying the night in my hospital room to driving me to the stadium for rehab, you were there for me from start to finish.

My life became front-page news during this ordeal. I'd like to thank all who helped Heidi and me remain, literally, guarded during this difficult time. From team security to the North Attleboro Police Department, you all were tremendous. Brad Blank, thanks for being a mensch. And a special thank-you to Michael Holley. Working with you has been an honor.

To all of the wonderful people at the American Stroke Association, your efforts to educate America about stroke and its warning signs are remarkable. To all of the members of Tedy's

Team, you have made such a difference and are true inspirations to me. I admire every one of you.

To all of you out there who gave me the support I needed to face the biggest challenge of my life, this wouldn't have been possible alone. I needed your letters, I needed your e-mails, I needed every word of encouragement I received. I needed your prayers. Thank you all and God bless.

PROLOGUE

I should have known that the first Sunday in February 2005 was going to be one of the best of my career, because it began perfectly. It was two hours before the kickoff of Super Bowl XXXIX, and I was on the field, happily scanning the Alltel Stadium seats. I found the family section of the half-empty stadium and ran toward my wife, Heidi, who was with two of our three sons. I've been to four Super Bowls with the New England Patriots, so I know that the final game of the year is not only the longest and has the longest halftime show of the year, it's also the longest *pre*-game wait of the year. After a while, anxious players and devoted fans just want the action to start. Imagine my boys, both under five years old at the time, sitting patiently with Heidi for two hours. I ran to their section and did something that I'll never take for granted again: I picked up my sons and brought them to the field so I could run and play with them.

Dante was four weeks old then, so he was back at the team

hotel with a family friend who was kind enough to babysit. But there I was with Tedy Jr.—we call him TJ—and Rex, chasing and being chased. The first thing both of them did was run to the end zone and peer into a tiny camera that was near the pylon. Then they ran after me as I backpedaled toward the logos of the Patriots and the Philadelphia Eagles. We ran and wrestled for about fifteen minutes before it was time for them to go back to their seats. I don't know why, but I've always been able to flip the switch pretty quickly. It doesn't take me long to go from a thirty-four-year-old loving father who laughs with his sons to a thirty-four-year-old middle linebacker who violently collides with guards, fullbacks, and running backs. The pre-game run was great for all of us: Heidi got a little break from the boys, TJ and Rex were able to burn off some energy, and I was able to relax before a game that would establish our team as one of the best in National Football League history.

We had won two of the previous three Super Bowls, in New Orleans and Houston, and were confident that we could make it three out of four in Jacksonville, Florida. It wasn't cockiness. You just have to understand the level of talent, trust, and accountability we had on our team. It started with the things that everybody could see: we had already rolled to January play-off wins over the Indianapolis Colts and the Pittsburgh Steelers. We played the Colts in the New England snow (I love playing in bad-weather games) and held their powerful offense to 3 points. We scored 41 points on the Steelers, who had beaten us in October and had lost just one game the entire season. We had been in a lot of hyped, nationally televised games and we knew how to play in them.

But it was more than that. It was the little things we did on the field and in the locker room. In the Pittsburgh game, for example, the Steelers were trying to convert a 4th-and-1 play in the first quarter. Bill Belichick called Ted Johnson and me to the sideline. Belichick, who has a reputation as one of the smartest head coaches in pro football, gave us brilliant instructions. "Roscoe Lena the nose," he shouted. That's football jargon, but what he was telling us to do was move the nose tackle to the side of the ball where we thought the Steelers were going to run. Ted and I weren't thinking that way on our own. As linebackers, we were thinking that we needed to get a little closer to the line of scrimmage or maybe dive over a guy to stop the run. And there was Belichick telling us to move the nose tackle so we could get more penetration. It was smart football and it worked: we stopped the Steelers on that play, forced them to fumble, and took control of the AFC Championship Game by halftime. It was the win that earned us the trip to Jacksonville. Obviously I didn't know it at the time, but my life would be forever changed ten days after the Super Bowl, and later I would be amazed at just how intelligent and measured Belichick can be.

We had a lot of experienced players on our team, so we continually pushed one another. Willie McGinest would make sure he was the first player in the weight room. If you walked in 10 or 15 minutes after him, he'd stare at an imaginary watch and say, "You're rolling in a little late. Someone decided to sleep in today?" Rodney Harrison would always police the defensive backs. He'd tell them how to play, how to study game film, even how much rest they should be getting at night. All of us would chastise a player if we thought he was taking a "shower pill"—a quick shower for a quick getaway—after practice. "Oh, you're not watching extra film today?" one of us would say. "I'm not leaving for another two hours." We also had an important mantra: never sell each other out. Romeo Crennel, our defensive coordinator for four years, emphasized clear and unified communication. He told us that even if we make a wrong call on the field, just make sure we're all wrong together.

It truly was a great team, one that I honestly felt could not be beaten that postseason. I happened to be playing the best football of my career and had been selected to play in my first Pro Bowl. The members of our defense believed that we could force Philadelphia to play on our terms. The Eagles employed the West Coast offense, which is based on a lot of timing routes. We thought that we could anticipate the patterns of the receivers and running backs, reroute them—just as we had against the Colts—and overpower their team with our physical style. Players usually don't like when coaches add new twists to the game plan twenty-four hours before a game, especially the Super Bowl, but we added some late new wrinkles to catch Philadelphia off guard.

One of the defenses was called Dolphin, which is when both inside linebackers are responsible for the "A" gap. Essentially, Mike Vrabel and I had the freedom to flip-flop: he could shoot the gap and I would have the running back in man-to-man coverage, or vice versa. We had such confidence in each other that we often wouldn't decide which of us would rush until just before the ball was snapped. I'd look at the backfield formation and quickly say to Mike, "Okay, you go." Or he'd do the same to me. Mike, who is one of my best friends on the team, actually caught a touchdown pass in the game when he was lined up as a tight end. I had a sack, 7 tackles, and an interception. Rodney had 2 interceptions, with the second one securing both the game and a *Sports Illustrated* cover shot. Another key (and often overlooked) play was Josh Miller's punt in the fourth quarter that pinned the Eagles inside the 5-yard line. We won the game, 24–21.

To kick off the celebration, I grabbed a huge bucket of water and dumped it on Belichick, who was sharing a sweet moment with his father, Steve. I've got a soft spot for family scenes like that, because my family is so important to me. As soon as the game was over, TJ and Rex were back on the field, accompanied by Heidi and my sister, Natalia. The boys were pushing an inflatable Super Bowl trophy that was on the field, and when the real Lombardi Trophy was passed our way, TJ actually licked it. I've still got the picture of him putting his tongue on the trophy. After the on-field celebration, everyone went to the party at our team hotel. The trophy was on a stage where the entertainment for the night was going to perform. I took it and got pictures with everyone: Heidi and me with the trophy; my brother, my sister, and me, with the trophy; Heidi, my mom, and me with the trophy—it went on for a while. I was so happy. As I was finishing with the pictures, Lionel Richie started singing. I went onstage as he sang and put the trophy back where I got it. He looked at me like, "Who is this guy?" And then Heidi and I danced to "Penny Lover."

I must have gone to bed at four in the morning, and I was awake a few hours later to do *Good Morning America* along with Deion Branch, who was the MVP of the game. At least I had more rest than some guys, who didn't sleep at all. I'll never forget some of the silly stuff that took place on the plane back to Boston.

While the players who were hungover slept, the players who were still in party mode decided to play some jokes. If you were asleep with your mouth open, watch out: you were a candidate to get mayonnaise on your lips. That's what happened to Dan Koppen, our starting center. It was worse for Vrabel; someone put butter on his lips. I don't know how he slept through it, but only a few minutes later he wiped his mouth and some of the butter fell onto his custom-made suit. He was furious. He stalked around the plane, searching for anyone who seemed to be smirking or looking on suspiciously. "Who did it?" he shouted, carrying a Gatorade bottle. "Who wants a Gatorade shower?" No one said anything. Larry Izzo had his video camera and recorded the whole thing.

Another season was over, and for the second year in a row we had won our final game. There wasn't a sense that we were finished as a group, either. We had a good mix of young guys and veterans, we had a great quarterback in Tom Brady, and we were well managed and well coached.

At home, Heidi and I knew that we were blessed. We had a beautiful family and were comfortable living in North Attleboro, Massachusetts. We weren't living there by coincidence. We'd always felt that it was our community, some of our best friends were there, and we often talked of sending our kids to the public schools. I had been able to play my entire career with one franchise and become one of the most popular Patriots in team history. I would be instantly humbled and flattered whenever I saw anyone wearing a number 54 "Bruschi" jersey, because I think the ultimate compliment is for someone to put your name on his back.

For the third February in four years, we had a parade through the streets of downtown Boston. It was awesome to see thousands of people cheering, waving, and holding up signs for us. After the parade, the Pro Bowl participants went to a minibus that took us to a luxury plane, our transportation to Honolulu for the game. At times we had to remind ourselves that we were actually on a plane, because it was incredible with its sectional couch, lounge chairs, kitchen table, dining room, bedroom, and two showers. We played Trivial Pursuit most of the way to Hawaii—it's a great game that can be played forever as long as no one gets all the right answers.

Just before the start of the Pro Bowl, the Patriots players had a private moment in the AFC locker room. I remember Brady talking about winning three Super Bowls in a row. He mentioned that it had never been done before and that we needed to be the team to do it. On that day, February 13, 2005, winning three in a row represented the biggest and most immediate challenge of my career.

A few mornings later, I awoke at four o'clock with what I thought was a headache. At six, the headache intensified and I lost my balance. Shortly after ten, I found myself in an ambulance on the way to Massachusetts General Hospital so I could learn what was happening to me. My perspective would change, literally and figuratively; I found myself questioning if my vision, which was normally better than 20/20, would fully return. Everything I stood for would be challenged, and my faith and my marriage would be tested. Not only was my career in jeopardy, I thought it was over.

Just two weeks after playing in the Super Bowl, I remember sitting at our small kitchen table and telling my family that I couldn't play anymore. I told Belichick the same thing a couple weeks later in his Gillette Stadium office, on a day when Heidi had to drive me to that office because I couldn't see well enough to do it myself. There was even a six-week period when my doctors forbade me from doing something that many fathers do instinctively. It was something I had done hundreds of times at home and once on Super Bowl Sunday: run to my boys and simply pick them up.

1

TEDY BRUSCHI, LINEBACKER

've been a pro football player for twelve years, and my end-of-season story hasn't changed in a decade: it's always been tough for me to fall asleep when there are no more games to play. You get used to the frantic NFL schedule, one that's akin to cramming for sixteen different tests in sixteen weeks. There are workouts and meetings in the mornings, practices in the afternoons, and extra film study in the evenings. There is a lot of information to absorb in a short amount of time, all leading to the ultimate high of playing in a game once a week. It usually takes my body a few weeks to adjust to the off-season schedule. This explains why, one day after I returned from the 2005 Pro Bowl, the late-night glow from a television could be seen in the master bedroom at 21 Red Oak Road. It was one o'clock in the morning, and as Heidi slept, I sat in bed watching a repeat. Not only was it a repeat that many fans in America had recently seen, it was a program in which I had been one of the characters.

The NFL Network was showing a replay of our conference championship win over the Pittsburgh Steelers. The game replay reminded me how punishing parts of that afternoon were, especially one collision that I had with Jerome Bettis. My playing weight is about 245 pounds, and Bettis is one of the few running backs who actually outweighs me—by at least 10 pounds and most likely 15. There was a play when he rumbled through the hole and I met him there. It was force against force; we both fell to the ground, and we both bounced up promising to be in the other's face all day.

The play was so vivid that I dreamed about it when I finally dozed off. In my dream, Bettis was running toward me. And there I was getting ready to wrap him up and make the sure tackle. This time there was no playful trash talking at the end of the play. This time my muscles contracted and there was tightness in my neck. My fists were clenched and my arms were in the air, as if I were bracing for something big. That's how I awoke at 4 A.M. It was no longer a dream; there certainly was something odd about my left arm and left leg. When you play pro football, you get used to playing in pain and waking up sore. You really do develop a threshold for pain, and when you're on the field you tell yourself that it will go away in twenty seconds. So I stayed in bed for a few minutes, trying to make a fist and regain the strength in my arm. It never occurred to me that something was really wrong.

That night, as usual, I slept to Heidi's right, the side of the bed closest to two windows in our bedroom. As I got up to use the bathroom, I noticed that the numbness in my leg was more problematic than I had thought. The "walk" to the bathroom never happened. I tried to stand and lost my balance. I grabbed a post at the foot of the bed, saving me from crashing into the windows. But the sudden grabbing of the bed and the commotion to keep myself standing was enough to awaken a confused Heidi.

"What are you doing?" she asked.

"I think I slept on my arm wrong or something," I answered.

Neither of us was processing what the other was saying. It was too early, and we were both disoriented. Heidi told me to get back in bed, and I told her I would after I went to the bathroom. But my sleeping left leg and left arm wouldn't cooperate, so I got down on my hands and knees and crawled to the bathroom. Once there, I obviously couldn't stand. I sat on the toilet for a few seconds. I had to hold myself there until I was finished, and then I sat there trying to figure out how I was going to get back to bed. It seems so clear telling the story now. Now I know that I should have been more concerned earlier. All the symptoms were there: no balance, numbness, muscle weakness, and the early stages of a headache. But that night, I just sat on the toilet, wondering if all of it had happened because I had slept awkwardly. I must have been in there for ten or fifteen minutes, because Heidi woke up again.

"Are you okay?" she asked.

"I think I slept on my arm or something, and now I've got a headache," I replied, still sitting in the bathroom.

"Maybe you were sleepwalking," she said. "Come back to bed."

I did go back to bed—through the air. I wasn't confident that I could make the short walk from the bathroom, so I took a step out and leaped. I dived in, landed sideways, and slept that way for the next hour before waking up again. This time the headache was stronger than before, and I couldn't get comfortable. Heidi got some Tylenol, and after I took it I decided to sleep downstairs on the couch. But I had to make it downstairs. I sat on the edge of the stairs, like a small child who hasn't quite mastered walking, and slid to the bottom. I made another dive, this time for the couch, and slept there. Briefly.

There have been many rough, sleepless nights in my NFL career. There are times when a shoulder is so tender that even rolling over brings a great deal of pain. But the early-morning hours of February 15 were different because there were so many moving parts: the inexplicable headache, the lack of balance and coordination, numbness on the left side of my body. I took an Aleve and, surprisingly, had a much easier time walking up the stairs and getting into bed. I fell asleep, and ninety minutes later Heidi let me rest when the boys awoke at six-thirty.

Heidi may have closed the door so I could sleep uninterrupted, but the incidents at 4 and 5 A.M. stayed with her as she fed the boys. She often says that she knows me better than I know myself, and she's right. She has watched me play football since my days at the University of Arizona, so she knows the difference between football discomfort and something else. This was clearly something else, so Heidi was eager to talk to her father, Bill Bomberger, who is a physician's assistant in Tucson. We're always asking Bill for medical advice, and he's always willing to help. Much later, Bill would scold us for waiting until 10 A.M. on the East Coast—seven in Arizona—before calling him. Heidi explained that she didn't want to wake him up too early. Besides, neither of us ever imagined that February 15 would be one of our longest days of 2005, one that we'd never forget for the rest of our lives. Heidi told her father that some strange things had been going on with me in the middle of the night. She described my symptoms, and Bill came to a swift conclusion: I needed to be seen immediately.

While Heidi was downstairs on the phone, I was in the bedroom waking up. I moved to the edge of the bed and just sat there, staring. For the first time that morning, I was scared. I didn't know what was happening to me, but I knew it had nothing to do with football. The thrashing headache was still there, and I was starting to have problems with my vision. Heidi entered the room to tell me that I needed to go to the hospital. I didn't need to be convinced. By then, I was so shaken by what was going on that I wanted to go. I called the Patriots' head trainer, Jim Whalen. He heard what I had to say and told me to call 911 while he contacted some people at Massachusetts General Hospital. In the meantime, our oldest son ran into the room with his usual enthusiasm and said, "Good morning, Daddy." I could hear TJ, but I couldn't see him. And then—*boom*—there he was on my right side. I saw him so suddenly that he startled me. That's when I looked at Heidi and said, "Call 911."

I've known Heidi since she was a freshman volleyball player at Arizona and I was a redshirt sophomore playing defensive line on the football team. We know how to read each other's emotions without saying much at all, so I know she was screaming inside when she somehow managed to make a composed 911 call and then follow it with a call to close friends who could take care of the kids. She contacted Tracie Pond, one of our North

Attleboro neighbors. Tracie has three kids of her own, but she was quickly at our house. Fortunately for us, her mother was visiting, and that allowed her to help us. And we needed it. Dante was just an infant at the time and was still being nursed. Heidi considered taking him with us to the hospital, but Tracie said it wasn't necessary. She told us not to worry; she had stayed with the boys before and it wouldn't be a problem this time.

The day already felt full and it was well before noon. I couldn't even speculate on what my issue was. As far as I knew I was a healthy thirty-one-year-old middle linebacker. I had played in the Super Bowl ten days earlier and in the Pro Bowl in the previous thirty-six hours. And just like that there was an ambulance at my house, waiting to take me to the hospital. I was given a vision test, and it was quickly apparent that my results were poor. I remember the EMT saying, "Let me know when you can see my finger." He moved his index finger from left to right and then right to left. Whenever he moved it to the left, I saw nothing but blackness.

I was placed in a chair, which became a stretcher, and carried outside. It was midmorning on a weekday, so there weren't many people around. It was mostly quiet on the street, but you could hear the pavement echoing with the footsteps of two running boys—my sons. The boys had been with Tracie, who told them that Mommy and Daddy were going away for a little trip. We might have been preparing to go to the hospital, but we never mentioned the word to them. But when TJ saw the red and white lights flashing and me on a stretcher, he ran outside.

On an ordinary day, we'd all go to the end of the cul-de-sac and the boys would play and ride their bikes. I'm sure my sons were too young to grasp that something was wrong and that I was starting to worry. Heidi was trying her best to be upbeat. She told TJ and Rex, who had run out after TJ, that Daddy was going for a ride. They really are wonderful boys, and they brought some levity to the situation by saying, "Good-bye, Daddy. Have fun." I'm an emotional guy who rarely shows it through tears, but I was crying when I saw my boys. I picked them up and pulled them close to me. I kissed them both and told them, over and over, how much I loved them. And then the doors closed for the thirty-five-minute trip to Boston.

Heidi was in the back of the ambulance with me and tried to be positive as she held my hand. I had my cell phone and called Jim Whalen twice more. "What's wrong with me, Jim?" I asked. "What's going on?" He didn't know, but he had already spoken with people who had a good idea. I was a few minutes away from meeting David Greer, a neurologist at Mass General. An emergency room physician had called Dr. Greer and told him a Patriots player was on his way to the hospital. It was fitting, because Dr. Greer was in the process of completing the paperwork that would make him the chief neurologist for the Patriots and the Red Sox. He cleared his schedule for the next three days and focused on trying to get me back to health.

My arrival at the hospital overwhelmed me. It may sound silly, but after seeing all of the sick people in the ER, it began to register that I was sick, too. It seemed so improbable. I remember being rushed to a room with a sliding glass door, and as I lay there on a gurney, I was surrounded by what seemed like dozens of men in white coats.

"What's going on here?" I asked no one in particular. "Who are all of you?"

There were residents from neurology and emergency medicine. There was a stroke fellow. There was a cardiologist. As they examined me and asked questions, Heidi moved around the table, trying to answer the questions that I couldn't. She also had the presence of mind to ask who they were and to write down all of the important things they had to say. Things were happening very quickly, so much so that in the emergency room I actually had an echocardiogram and an ultrasound of my heart. Dr. Greer told me later that those things rarely happen so fast. But it wasn't what he told me months later that stunned me. It's what he said in the eleven o'clock hour on the fifteenth that took me aback. He stood next to my stretcher, put his hand on my shoulder, and said, "Tedy, you've had a stroke."

A stroke? I was shocked. How could I have had a stroke? I actually asked this decorated neurologist—who comes from a family of doctors and even has a master's in English—if he was sure. Heidi put her face in her hands and began to cry. When she heard the word *stroke*, she immediately thought "debilitating." Naturally, we both wondered if I would ever be the same. By the time I was seen by Dr. Greer, the symptoms were obvious. There was drooping on the left side of my face, and I had sensory and coordination problems on the left side of my body. When I looked to the left out of either eye, there was darkness. And there was that pounding headache, much more intense than it had been at any point at home. The headache was so strong that I slowly stopped responding to the doctors' questions. I was in the fetal position, just hoping for relief.

For Dr. Greer and the medical team, the focus was on finding answers. All of the terms they used that day were unfamiliar to me then but are part of my vocabulary today. The first question was simple: was my stroke bleeding or not? A CAT scan determined that it wasn't. Since my first symptoms had taken place well over three hours before I arrived at the hospital, I couldn't be given a clot-busting medicine called TPA (tissue plasminogen activator) that can sometimes open the blood vessels. The drug is not given to those who have had hemorrhagic (bleeding) strokes because it can induce further bleeding.

Heidi and I were getting a crash course on stroke as I was experiencing one. We would learn that a stroke is caused by the blockage of a blood vessel, sometimes by a clot and sometimes by the narrowing of a vessel. What concerned the doctors about me was the weakness on the left side of my body. To them, it meant that there was a circulation problem in the back of my head. They were sensitive to that because there is one main blood vessel—the basilar artery—that leads to the back of the brain. If it is clogged, the results are fatal 80 percent of the time. So I was given a CT angiogram, which is when dye is injected into the veins and travels to the brain. Pictures are then taken of the brain to see if all the vessels are open and if there are any residual clots ready to do some damage. I didn't have any problems there, nor did I have a dissection, which is when there is a tear in a blood vessel. But there was more surprising news to come: I had a hole in my heart.

The hole had been there since birth, and it was allowing blood to travel freely between the ventricles. It was the cause of my stroke. A clot had formed and gone toward the back of the right side of my brain. Looking back on it now, I was lucky. The stroke could have been larger, and the trouble area in my brain could have been farther back. If that had been the case, some of my motor skills and vision would not have returned. I feel blessed now, but I didn't have that perspective at the time. I had been told that I had a stroke and that there was a hole in my heart that might require surgery at another time. I also couldn't see and had to be observed closely because there was the likelihood of another stroke over the next two weeks.

"Is there anything else?" I asked my doctors.

I wanted to make sure they weren't leaving anything out, that they weren't trying to craft a diplomatic way to give me more alarming news. I remember Heidi saying that it seemed like we were in a movie, and I felt the same way. Long before the stroke, I had supported Mass General and the Spaulding Rehabilitation Hospital. When I talk to people now, I tell them that the hospital they see as someone else's can be theirs tomorrow. That's what happened to me. I never expected to be in Boston on that Wednesday morning. I know it was tough for my wife to watch me take all those tests and, in a few cases, watch me struggle with them. My speech wasn't slurred, but my handwriting tests weren't very good. My personality hadn't changed—which often happens with stroke survivors—but I wasn't walking like myself. And I know it took a lot of strength for Heidi not to panic when she saw all the things I was missing on my vision tests. I didn't think of football the first two days. Long term, I wanted to know what it was going to take to recover. Short term, honestly, I just wanted to get rid of the headache.

We were fortunate to be in the care of a doctor who was as

charismatic as he was competent. I would learn later that the old joke about neurologists is that they are so serious and protective that they want you to wear a helmet while driving a car. That was far from Dr. Greer's profile. His terrific sense of humor was apparent early, even in a moment of crisis. As he pushed me around in a wheelchair, going from test to test, he told me that he had to get me out of the hospital as soon as possible because "I'm used to being the biggest person on this floor and you're bigger than me. I don't like that." You want excellent care when you're sick and you want someone whose personality can put you at ease. Dr. Greer provided that for Heidi and me. We looked forward to seeing this young, athletic doctor—he was in his late thirties—walk in the door, even when he was coming to give a test. Somehow, he was able to bring humor to those occasions as well.

To test my short-term memory, Dr. Greer told me to remember three words: "yellow," "mailman," and "honesty." He would talk for a few minutes and say, "Tedy, do you remember those words I gave you?" I said I did. Later, Dr. Greer would say that he always uses the same three words with patients because he'd have problems remembering them himself. He was clearly the best man for a bad situation, a man who gained our trust and made us smile.

By dinnertime on day one, I told Heidi to go home. There was nothing more she could do at the hospital, and Jim Whalen and Dave Granito of the Patriots offered to be there if anything went wrong. So Heidi left. But after some great friends of ours helped put TJ and Rex to bed and Heidi nursed Dante in the middle of the night, she returned to the hospital at three the next morning. Dave had told Heidi to call him on his cell if she needed anything. True to his word, he was there to take her to the hospital at an hour when most people sleep through their ringing cell phones or turn them off.

I was in physical pain at the hospital, but the emotional hurt began to sink in as well. When I saw Jim, I verbalized what seemed to be obvious: "Jim, you'll probably never tape my ankles again."

He heard what I had to say, but he was in no hurry to agree with me. He paused and said, "You might be right, Tedy. We don't know that yet."

The story had long gone public by then, with several news outlets guessing what the problem was. There were some reports that I had an aneurysm, and some said I had a bleeding stroke. Stacey James, the Patriots' media relations director, asked if I wanted to release a statement confirming that I had had a stroke.

"Write something up, let me look at it, and then I'll okay it," I told him.

I wasn't ashamed of anything. I had had a stroke, and I understood that a lot of people—including myself in February 2005—were uneducated about what that meant. I wasn't sure what the public had to say, but I do know that the people closest to me immediately offered their support. My brother, Tony, and his wife, Linda, live in Las Vegas, and they flew to New England as soon as they heard the news. Heidi's mother and sister—Vicki and Kati—flew out from Tucson. There were so many visitors from the Patriots that, on the second day, my floor was locked down because the doctors said I couldn't possibly get any rest with all the people who wanted to see me. I was able to see the owner of the team, Robert Kraft, and his wife, Myra. Scott Pioli, the team's top personnel man, was there early. A lot of players—Jarvis Green, Rodney Bailey, Deion Branch— stopped by and saw me, while others were turned away. Heidi was in control of my cell phone and hers, and both phones rang constantly. I think I scared Jarvis the first time he saw me: he walked in during a time when IVs were being put into me, and I think it hit him that I was in bad shape.

The first time I saw my brother, I was in a wheelchair. We both broke down and hugged. He kept telling me that I was going to be all right, and I repeated the words to him. I was still in pain; doctors had to be very discriminating with what they gave me for my headache because they didn't want the stroke to bleed. I say I had a headache, but that's because I don't have another word for the thrashing and pounding that was going on inside my head. When the pain was at its strongest, I didn't care about food and I couldn't engage in an extended conversation. It was a pain unlike any I had experienced, a headache so intense that even whispers seemed like screams.

A lot of things in the hospital were a blur my first thirty-six hours there, but I remember in great detail a moment when I wanted to punch a cardiologist in the face. I hadn't been in the hospital more than a few hours when Dr. Adolph Hutter, the Patriots' cardiologist and a man whom I like, came up to me and said, "Don't worry, Tedy, we'll get you back on the field in no time." I couldn't believe it. Being on the field was the last thing on my mind, and here he was practically slapping me on my butt. I would tease Dr. Hutter about it later, but it was a comment that annoyed me at the time.

Was I going to be all right? I believed that I would be able to get better, well enough to live a normal life with my wife and children. I didn't believe that playing football again was a reasonable option; I had had a stroke—how was I supposed to play football? And if my eyes weren't going to be the same—and there was no guarantee that they would—there was no way anyone would allow me to play in the NFL. I was in a different place now, far from Gillette Stadium where the types of tests I usually take are conditioning tests in July. For those, linebackers have to perform two sets of ten 50-yard sprints, with each sprint completed in seven seconds or fewer. When I was in the hospital, my tests would have seemed basic to the typical pro football player and challenging to the typical stroke survivor. I would take walks with physical and occupational therapists, down the hall and back. The contrast between what my life used to be and what it was going to be was amazing. I was used to working with my hands, being coordinated enough to "shed" blocks and pluck stray footballs out of the air. In the hospital, I would try to do something as simple as writing, but my fingers wouldn't do what my brain told them to. It was humbling, frustrating, and, at times, depressing.

Dr. Greer had several things to be concerned about in those first few days. While he wanted me to be seen quickly, he also wanted to slow down the process. His philosophy is that when people get special care, they sometimes get inappropriate care. He wanted to be decisive without being rash. In fact, he waited two days before agreeing that the proper way to fix the hole in my heart was through a catheterization procedure that would take place in March. And while Heidi commented early on that it seemed like we were in a movie, her words were proving to be prophetic. The hospital scene was chaotic. It seemed that my door was opening every few seconds for another test or exercise. My major pain pill my second day there was Percocet, but I was just beginning to scratch the surface with shots and medications.

Things weren't normal for Dr. Greer, either. He has been around doctors his entire life—his father was the University of Florida's chairman of neurology for thirty-eight years—so he has an extremely strong sense of how things should go and patients should be treated; he doesn't believe that one person's health is more important than another's. So while he was great to me, he was great to his other patients as well. His beeper went off every fifteen minutes the first two days I was in the hospital. His attention to me took him away from other patients, and he gave me a hard time, tongue in cheek, about that as well.

I didn't realize it then, but in the next few months I was going to learn about prescriptions that had never crossed my mind. And Dr. Greer was going to become more than a doctor for us. He would be a friend, a confidant, and an adviser. Just before I left the hospital, he also tried to cheer me up. He told me I would gradually get better, that the younger the patient is, the better chance he or she has of a full recovery. He was honest. He said he would make no promises about football, because he didn't know if my coordination level would be the same. I listened, but I was unrealistic: I wanted the improvement to happen immediately, and when it didn't, it got to me. One of my flaws is that I'm impatient. I don't always let things run their course, when in many cases, that's exactly what needs to happen.

Heidi had a cot next to my bed, and both of us found it difficult to sleep in the three days we were at Mass General. On day three, the day of my release, I knew there was a lot of work to be done. Yes, I was going home. But I was going to be visited there every day for two weeks by a nurse. On some days I was going to have to take three pills, and on others it would be as many as ten. I was going to need surgery soon, and there were going to be physical and psychological changes that would not only provide individual challenges, they would set forth the most serious challenge to my marriage. There were some business decisions to be made once I got home. Who was I going to be beyond Tedy Bruschi, linebacker? What kind of physical restrictions would I have to accept after the stroke? What was I going to do next?

When I was released from the hospital, television cameras and news photographers stood outside waiting for me. I had been told that I could go out of a back entrance and avoid the media, or I could leave out front and acknowledge the cameras. I was in a wheelchair until I reached the front, and then I walked out with Heidi. I squeezed her hand and told her not to let me fall. I tried my best to walk normally, but I was far from myself. Anne McCarthy Jacobson, who would become my physical therapist a few weeks later, was watching my exit from the hospital on TV. She told me later that she jotted down some notes after watching me walk: *He's lost visual field in both of his eyes and he's not rotating his head. He's not bending his hips and knees, and he's walking robotically. He's holding his wife's hand because he does not have control. He is very hesitant and he is not scanning visually*

*all the way to his left. His wife is guiding him to the car, and I sus-
pect it's a combination of balance and vision.*

I wasn't the same man, and I knew it as soon as I headed to
the car. Tony was driving and Linda was already in the front seat.
But when I first went to the car, I didn't see Linda sitting there.
I opened the passenger door expecting an empty seat, but Linda
was there and I hadn't seen anyone before. I gingerly sat in the
back with Heidi.

"Tony, drive the best that you can, man," I said to my
brother as he pulled away from the crowd. "Be smooth, please."

The motion of the car was killing me. I felt every small bump
in the road. I had a long way to go before I could think about
the way I used to be. But as we drove home, I was grateful for
so many things, starting with the health that I did have. I had
been told that I would have to be maintained on Coumadin, a
blood thinner, until at least June. I would have to start physical
therapy immediately to attempt to bring my body back. And I
knew that I would be returning to the hospital in about three
weeks for the patent foramen ovale (PFO) procedure to fix the
hole in my heart.

I was also appreciative of all the help and support I'd received
in the past three days. Tracie Pond stayed with our kids the first
day, and our neighbors Sharon and Bill Roberts relieved her
when they got home in the evening. In addition to the hospital
visits, we received several phone calls from teammates, friends,
and family members. The North Attleboro post office was great:
there were hundreds of letters simply marked "Tedy Bruschi,
North Attleboro, MA," yet they were still delivered to me.

At home, I was moved that Tony, Linda, Vicki, and Kati had come to town in the middle of the week on such short notice. After I rested for a few hours, I walked into our kitchen and sat at a small yellow table, a classic table for two that Heidi and I used for our family of five. I was the only one sitting as my brother and his wife, my in-laws, and Heidi stood around me. In our intimate circle, I tried my best to recap what had happened over the previous three days, put things in perspective, and thank them all. I told them that they were like angels to Heidi and me, and that's when emotion took over. It was hard for me to say it, but through the tears I was able to tell them that my football career was over.

We all cried, and they told me that they didn't care about football. They talked about the career I had enjoyed and how I had been blessed to play in a Pro Bowl and be part of three Super Bowl championship teams. We all agreed that I should be thankful that I had my faculties and was projected to get better, because there are many stroke survivors who couldn't say that.

Some people, really wise people, have the ability to see the big picture even when they are in the middle of a crisis. I've never been like that. If I'm seeing that big picture, it's a black-and-white photo; I don't seek out gray areas. Or, I should say, I didn't seek out shades of gray until the stroke forced me to.

In the first few weeks after the stroke, I would make what I thought were clear-cut decisions—and have them unfold nothing like I thought they would. I would soon inspire people and be inspired by people I hadn't known. I would also have days in which I wandered about, an emotionally fragile man who needed encouragement by the hour. It was a life-changing sequence that brought new meaning to that sports cliché "A lot of fans are counting on you."

A lot of fans were counting on me and relying on me, but not because of anything that took place on a field. They were stroke survivors who needed my answers because they needed to make sense of what was happening to them. These were people who needed answers to survive, people who would ask over and over, "How did you do it, Tedy? How did you get through?" The stroke was a marker on my personal timeline, an event that taught me new things about myself, and something that made me think deeply about my future and my past.

2

GROWING UP
IN CALI

To fully understand who I am, you have to start out West. Actually, the complex is called Freedom West, and it's at the corner of Golden Gate Avenue and Gough Street in San Francisco. It's one of those neighborhoods where you can glance in any direction and find someone who doesn't look like you. When I was growing up there, it was truly a cross-section of the city. My family lived in a duplex, which was one block away from the projects. Our neighbors to the right were black, our neighbors to the left were Latino, and the neighbors a few doors down were Chinese. Once my father moved out—my parents got divorced when I was five—a lot of people didn't know what the ethnic story was with us. My siblings and I got all kinds of guesses: *Mexican? Samoan? Indian? Hawaiian? What are you?*

The answer is that the three of us—Tony is the oldest, I'm in the middle, and Natalia is the youngest—are the children of an Italian father and a Filipina mother. Race and ethnicity weren't problems with any of my friends. I can imagine that their parents were consumed with the same topic as mine: money. It's no exaggeration to say that I learned about mortgages, car payments, and bankruptcies before I learned the intricacies of organized football. Both my mother and my father filed for bankruptcy at least once apiece, and probably more; I didn't really want to keep count. They had some hard times, financially and emotionally. They didn't have the most civil divorce, so when they communicated, most of their time was devoted to arguing. From my dad's perspective, it probably got worse when my mother remarried and my stepfather moved in with us. Almost as far back as I can remember—I think I was six or seven—there was always some stress regarding money. My mom would try to get as many jobs as she could and my stepfather had a job as well, but their combined income wasn't enough to erase the money worries.

Tony, Natalia, and I lived with my mother and stepfather during the week, and we visited my father, who lived about ten minutes away, on weekends. He spent a lot of time giving us his side of the story regarding the divorce, and when we returned home, my mother spent a lot of time giving us her view on my father. Man, it was ugly. I got along fine with my stepfather and didn't have any problems with him. But Tony, who is three years older than I am, had a tough time. He didn't like the living situation and got into trouble around the neighborhood, and my mother reached the point where she felt that she couldn't control him. There was a brief period when the kids were separated: Tony lived with my father (also named Tony) and Natalia and I stayed with my mom.

If you were to sit and talk with Tony and me today, you would think you were having a conversation with the same person; we really are identical people. But that wasn't the case when we were growing up. At times, we didn't like each other very much. A lot of it was a big brother versus little brother thing, where he got on my nerves and I got on his. We would fight all the time—we would really go at it—so when he went to live with my dad, it was good for both of us. I realized how much I missed him when he was gone, yet I was able to establish some independence without him.

As for Natalia, we were extremely close as kids. We are fourteen months apart, so we had some of the same friends and took the same bus—the 5 Fulton to the 22 Fillmore—to Marina Middle School. We started to grow apart in our early teens, naturally, because she was hanging out with her girlfriends and I was with the guys. I don't know if fighting runs in my family or not, but Natalia could defend herself when she needed to, just like Tony and me. I remember a couple of funny stories about her. There was a time when my mother wasn't feeling well and needed to rest. Natalia was talking on the phone in my mom's room and I said, "Natalia, get out of here. Mom's trying to sleep." She said something like, "I'm on the phone, Tedy. Leave me alone." So I snatched the phone out of her hand, hung it up, and told her to go somewhere else. *Boom!* She started to hit me. I thought, "Holy smoke; this girl's hitting me." I grabbed her, threw her on her bed, and ran to my room. I closed the door and she tried to break it down to get at me. There's no question she could take care of herself.

I guess I didn't learn my lesson, because a couple years later,

Natalia went off on me again. She was seeing a junior varsity football player at school, and I was a varsity senior. So when I saw the kid in the locker room, I threatened him and played the protective-brother role. You know: "I'll take care of you if you touch her. Stay away from her." When that got back to Natalia, whew, she was upset. She got in my face and told me to stay out of her business. That was the last time I did something like that.

We lived in San Francisco until I was thirteen. I had never played on a football team at that point. All of my football experience had taken place in neighborhood pickup games. There was a community circle of grass near our house that stretched on for about forty yards. I remember that it had a slight slope and there were sprinkler heads throughout that we tried to avoid (although my buddy busted up his knee on one during a game). We played football—tackle football—there most of the time, and sometimes we played up the street at Hayward Park. I didn't think there was anything special about the way I played football then, I just knew that when I did play I had a different mentality. You might say that I was the passive one compared to my brother, but I wasn't like that when I played. There was a kid in the neighborhood named Pepe. He bullied a lot of people, and it seemed like he bullied my entire family. He wasn't someone I would have normally taken on, but we were playing football one day and we got into it. I surprised myself: I punched him a few times and got him in a headlock. He wore a gold Playboy earring, and I can still see it popping out when I had him in that headlock. As I hit him I said, "This is for my sister. This is for my brother. And this is for me." Whenever I saw him after that,

I was a little nervous about what he was going to do. But he was cool after I checked him on the field.

Tony can probably tell twice as many fight stories as I can. And that was the problem as far as my mother was concerned. She felt that she needed to get us out of the city before we got into serious trouble. When Tony went to live with my father, it didn't go as well as planned. My father was a devoted Italian Catholic and we were all raised Catholic, so my father's idea was to send Tony to a private school called Sacred Heart. Dad thought Sacred Heart would straighten Tony out, but he got into more trouble there than he would have at a public school. So my mom told us we were all moving to Roseville during the second semester of my eighth-grade year.

When I heard "ville" I thought we were moving to a town with tumbleweeds in the streets, cowboy hats, and people walking around chewing on straw. Roseville? I had no idea that it was a part of Greater Sacramento, just over an hour away from San Francisco. It was completely different from Golden Gate and Gough in the city. It was a suburban place, and at first it seemed that we would be in a better financial situation there. I had my own room, and my mom talked about putting a pool in the backyard. But it wasn't long before my stepfather lost his job and there were more stressful conversations about money.

I'm not sure if it began in Roseville or San Francisco, but I started to become aware of the anger I had for people with certain attitudes. It would infuriate me when I sensed that someone thought they were better than me because of where they lived, what kind of clothes they wore, what kind of education they had, or what their parents did for a living. It wasn't always logical, but watching my parents struggle made me want to get back at the people who felt that they had some kind of financial entitlement. Maybe I was mad because my life wasn't very good and theirs appeared to be, or maybe it was the sense that they were looking down on me. It could have even been an incident that took place in middle school: I saw a group of kids playing football and I asked if I could play with them.

One kid, looking like a younger version of a J.Crew model, shook his head. "No, you can't play with us," he said. "You're too big."

I was the same size he was. And he knew me. In fact, all of those kids knew me. But there are times when you know that someone is keeping you out of a social circle simply because they think they're better than you. That was one of those times, and I'll never forget it. In any case, I've always felt like an underdog and have looked forward to opportunities where I can take out my anger on the so-called elite. At fourteen, I didn't realize that football would allow me to do exactly that for twenty years.

The first time I thought about organized football was at Roseville High's freshman orientation. I saw two friends of mine, Jason Ramsey and Eric Denio, and they motioned for me to sit next to them. I looked down at their feet and saw that they had cleats and water bottles with them.

"What are those for?" I asked them.

"Oh, we're trying out for the football team," one of them said. "You should come."

The next day I went out and played freshman football. Our coach's name was Don Hicks, and before practice he gave us a pep speech. He told us how good the practice was going to be and how excited he was about the season. Then he told us to break up into our positions. I didn't know where I was supposed to go because I had never taken the game that seriously. I asked Coach Hicks what I should do. He looked me up and down before finally saying, "Go with the linemen." And that's where I would be from high school all the way through college.

My father heard that I was playing football in Roseville, and he said he wanted to drive up from San Francisco to watch me practice. He always reminded me that he had coached everything from fishing to football and he would be able to tell what kind of player I was if he saw me. The first time he watched me practice, he came up to me afterward and said, "Ted, you got it. You got it." I was just a kid, so I didn't know what he was talking about when he started mentioning my pad level, my angles coming off the ball, and knowing how to use my body. I thought I was just playing a game, but my father saw something much greater from the start. What I started to see was that this game could be an equalizer for me. I could take on the private school kids, the rich kids, and the arrogant kids. I could compete with them without feeling that somebody was being given preferential treatment. It was the opposite of what I found during the middle school incident; kids were going to have to play against me if they wanted to win. No excuses. Football was the perfect meritocracy, a game that did you no favors based on wealth, education, or race. At that age, the football field was one of the only places where I felt I had a significant say in what would happen next.

Going into my sophomore year, Roseville moved from a smaller-school league, the Sierra Foothills League, to the bigger Capital Valley Conference. That meant we would have to play some of the city teams from Sacramento, not just the suburban schools. I viewed it as an exciting challenge, but some of the players on my team were scared. They thought we were going to get our butts kicked. I remember being angry when we scrimmaged the Sacramento schools. No one was keeping a formal score, but it was clear to me that we were holding our own; we could compete with anybody. Toward the end of one scrimmage, I wanted to send a message to the teammates who were timid. There was a running play, and I took an angle from my defensive tackle position and chased the back near the sideline. A long jump pit separated the football field from a gravel track. I got a perfect hit on the runner, sending him airborne, and he landed on the track. The hit was good, but the drama of the flight and cloud of dust from the track made it look even better. It seemed like everyone was watching, and you could hear the admiring "oohs" from players on both teams. Since it was the last play of the scrimmage, I ran to our sideline and shouted to our team, "I told you—we can beat anybody. Anybody on this team who doesn't believe in us, you need to get your mind right." That year we finished 10–0.

My father's words were turning out to be true. It certainly appeared that I had it when it came to playing football. A couple of things were starting to happen: recruiting letters from colleges were coming in, and I was emerging as one of my team's leaders. I never consciously set out to be a leader, but football was something I enjoyed doing. I didn't have a problem challenging teammates who didn't show enough passion or toughness. We once had a fumble drill in the rain where two guys were supposed to dive in the mud and fight for the ball. I thought it was great because I loved playing football in bad weather. As we were all lining up to do the drill, I heard two players behind me saying that they weren't going to do it. Their plan was to go through the motions and high-step through a mud pile without getting on the ground for the muddy ball. After I did the drill, I turned around to see if they were serious, and, sure enough, they were laughing and tiptoeing through the mud. I was furious. To me, just playing in the mud was half the fun, no matter who came up with the ball. But these guys seemed to believe they were above the rest of the team. I ran toward one of them and put my helmet in his chest. I lifted him and then put his back in the mud pile. I looked back to the other players in line and said, "Now everybody else had better dive for this ball."

By the time I was sixteen or seventeen, I think my issues with privilege were obvious. My teammates knew that I thought it was unacceptable if we lost to Jesuit High, a private school that we played often. To me, paying to go to school meant that you thought you were better than everyone else. Of course, I've met a lot of great people who attended private schools. I'm just telling you how adamant I was about it when I was a teenager. I've softened considerably on the issue, but it's still a touchy subject with me today. It's interesting, because my own sons now have everything that I never had when I was their age. I think that's why I'm so hard on them now; they don't always get everything they want.

Even though I did receive interest from colleges while in high school, I wasn't highly recruited. I visited three schools: Washington State, Arizona, and Brigham Young University. It was really a choice between the first two schools because I had always wanted to play in the Pac-10 Conference. When you grow up out West, the Pac-10 is number one in your mind, so that's where I wanted to be. Arizona felt right to me, and it should have. Some of the best decisions of my life were made there. On the football side it meant that I would play for a school that didn't get the same respect as USC or UCLA, and academically it wasn't perceived to be as prestigious as Stanford or Cal Berkeley. But being an outsider, athletically or economically, was nothing new to me. So the fact that I had a scholarship to a school that wasn't recognized as a perennial power didn't bother me. I knew there would be other players there with backgrounds similar to mine, players who never could have afforded to go to college if it hadn't been for football.

One day in August of my redshirt sophomore year, I walked with a few of those players into the weight room at Arizona's McKale Center. I didn't know it at the time, but it was the most significant workout I've ever had. I was talking and laughing with my friends, and I didn't know a freshman volleyball player was watching me. She didn't say anything to me then, but there was a frat party the next night and a lot of football players were there. I didn't go, but my buddy Jim Sprotte did. The volleyball player went up to him and said, "Is Tedy Bruschi here tonight?" Jim told me later that a girl had been asking about me at the party. "Well, is she cute?" I asked. Jim said that she was and gave me her number.

And that's how I met Heidi Bomberger, a girl who grew up in Auburn, Nebraska, a one-stoplight farming town. Her family moved to Tucson when she was ten. She was the Player of the

Year in Tucson her senior year of high school, and that led her to a volleyball scholarship at Arizona. I called her the day after Jim gave me her number, and I didn't regret it. I thought she was an engaging conversationalist, and it didn't hurt that she laughed at everything I said. I remember thinking, "Man, I'm a funny dude."

She was eighteen and I was twenty, and I kept saying to myself during the conversation, "This is going well. Really, really well. We seem to be on the same page a lot." There was one point in our conversation when I got another phone call and briefly picked up the other line. Heidi thought I was gone much longer than I was, because I heard part of her conversation with her roommate, Stephanie. I could hear Heidi saying, "I love his voice. Put on that song 'Sweet Thing' by Mary J. Blige." After hearing that I spoke up. "So, you like my voice, huh?" Heidi was embarrassed, but she also thought it was funny.

We talked on the phone the next day, and I liked her even more. She was playful, energetic, and smart. It was the same story the day after that. We had three good phone conversations and we still hadn't talked face-to-face. She had seen me, but I had no idea how she looked. I never had that blind-date nervousness about her, though. If you're a good friend of mine, I have a lot of trust in you, and that includes trusting your judgment. If Jim said Heidi was cute, then she was cute. I saw Heidi the fourth day at volleyball practice. I was walking down a ramp in McKale Center and saw the team stretching. I stood there so I could be seen, and after a few seconds, there was a tall girl with curly blond hair waving at me. When she was done with practice, we talked for the first time in person.

When I first started college, I wasn't looking for a serious girlfriend. But that mentality changed when I met Heidi. I knew she was what I was looking for. She was two years younger than I was, but she struck me as an accomplished woman. I was impressed that she was a good athlete and on scholarship. I liked her confidence and her personality, and my friend Jim was wrong: she wasn't just cute; she was the most amazing woman I had ever seen. I thought she was special and I knew I wanted to be in a relationship with her. I made her laugh when I told her that I wanted to take her out—but she would have to pick me up. The reason: the only mode of transportation I had was a used scooter I had bought with my Pell grant. So Heidi picked me up in her Toyota Celica, and at the end of the night, I asked her if I could have permission to hug her. We definitely eased into our relationship, but once we began it was obvious that it was going to last a long time. One of the first times Heidi met Tony, she said, "You know I'm going to marry your brother, right?"

While Heidi brought a great deal of joy and peace into my life, I still had a huge chip on my shoulder at that age. Heidi told me that she thought I had charisma when she first met me and that's one of the things she found attractive. But there's a fine line between being charismatic and being a jerk, and, honestly, I could be both. Take that chip on my shoulder, add alcohol to my body, and things just exploded in me. My whole mentality changed when I drank, and there were times I went crazy. I was very destructive. I started fights. I verbally abused people. I broke things. If the campus cops heard about a bunch of guys from the football team showing up at a party and causing trouble, they suspected the group I was with.

Honestly, there's still some shame as I share the stories about drinking. I hadn't evolved to the point I'm at now, where I don't drink at all. I was still five years away from quitting alcohol for the first time, and eight years away from stopping for good. My last drink came on one of the saddest days in American history, September 11, 2001.

Several members of the team had met at Drew Bledsoe's house that night, just to be together at such a confusing and strange time for our country. Late in the night, there were three of us remained in Drew's home theater: Drew, Tom Brady, and me. The quarterbacks thought I was going to watch a movie and crash there, something I had done many times. But I was able to sneak out—drunk—and drive home. It was a horrible decision. I called Tony on my way home, and he called Heidi, wondering why I was behind the wheel in that condition. Fortunately, I was able to make it home without hurting myself or anyone else. I wasn't sober, but I knew better than to go upstairs to bed. I slept on the couch that night and woke up to a disappointed Heidi standing over me.

"What's it going to be, Tedy?" she said. "How far is this going to go?"

She was holding a young TJ at the time and was pregnant with Rex. She was right. I was either going to accept responsibility or continue to be reckless. I felt that drinking was affecting my ability to be the father and husband I wanted to be, so I stopped. I won't drink again.

No matter how chaotic things became during my college days in Tucson, there was always one stabilizing force: my relationship with Heidi. She and I respected each other as athletes.

She watched my games and saw me set an NCAA record for career sacks. I watched her play volleyball, and when she wanted to walk on to Arizona's nationally ranked softball team, I watched her try out. She made it. (I still haven't seen anyone smile and run the bases like Heidi.) During my last two years at Arizona, when I played my best football, we both knew it was likely that an NFL team was going to draft me. I knew I was going to have to change positions in the pros because I was too small to play on the defensive line. Whenever the local reporters would ask me what NFL team I wanted to play for, I told them it didn't matter. When they'd press me I'd say, "Somewhere close." On the day of the 1996 draft, it was just the opposite. Heidi was in Washington State when I was drafted, so I watched the draft at our apartment with my stepfather and a couple of friends of mine. We were all talking in the third round when I was the only one who noticed the crawl on ESPN. I thought I saw my name on it and said, "Guys, I think I just got drafted by the Patriots." I knew how random the draft could be, but I never imagined I'd be playing in New England. When Heidi called the apartment to find out what happened, she was surprised, too. "New England?" she said. "Is that in the United States?"

Not only was it a part of the northeastern United States, New England was going to be my professional home for life if it were up to me. As a kid in San Francisco, I was a Dallas Cowboys fan—don't ask me how that happened. I loved the Cowboys until they fired Tom Landry, brought in Jimmy Johnson, and, a few years later, said good-bye to Johnson. It turned me off as a sports fan to watch so many different characters with my favorite team. I told myself that if I made it to the pros,

I wanted to be one of those guys who could be identified with one team.

All aspects of my life were about to change. The first time I talked to my new head coach, the legendary Bill Parcells, the phone conversation was brief. He said, "Tedy, we're going to use you at linebacker. Here's [linebackers coach] Al Groh." That was it. The message was clear: I was a professional now, and I had better be prepared to adjust quickly. I didn't know if I would be able to make it as a football player the rest of my life, but I did know the woman I wanted to be with for a lifetime. The day before I left Tucson for training camp in New England, I proposed to Heidi. We would get married after my rookie year, June 27, 1997. But before the marriage, there was other business to handle.

When I signed my first contract with the Patriots, I received a signing bonus of $285,000. It was the most money I had ever seen at once, and I had a plan for it. The first thing I needed to do was help my family with some bills. Then I thought about the value of homes and how powerful it is to have one of your own. My mother had always stressed that if I were ever in position to get a house, I should try my best to get it and pay it off. All I wanted as a rookie was $100,000 for a house. I told myself that if I played for just one year, I could buy a house and work at a gas station to make the payments. I know it sounds weird to hear me saying that, but the talk of mortgages and payments wore on me as a kid. During my first years in the league, my goal was to get to the point where I didn't have any payments to make at all. I wanted to see a house, write a check for it, and say, "Here's a check—get out of my face."

I put a down payment on a 1,800-square-foot, $157,000 house on the east side of Tucson my rookie year. And every time I got any money, it was put toward paying off the house entirely. Both Heidi's and my parents are real estate agents, so we felt we had good information on the housing market. My plan was to live in Tucson half the year and be in New England during football season. I was able to pay off the house within a year, and that's something I took a lot of pride in then and still do now. My teammates have joked with me about my "mattress philosophy," saying that all of my cash is stuffed in a bed somewhere. They know how conservative I am and how I don't want to hear about any risky moneymaking investments. A lot of them don't know how I became this way. It comes from being broke. I saw money problems eat up my mom, my dad, and my stepdad. I don't want that to happen to me. So I don't ever want a mortgage, and I don't care that it's a tax write-off.

I bought a house in Las Vegas, and I own the house I live in now. I own the pillars, the garage, the roof, and all the little pieces of wood. It's important to me. I remember what it was like for my family to owe everybody, and now it feels good not to owe anyone. Heidi and I have been blessed financially, but I still don't make lavish decisions with money. I've heard horror stories about players who have made a little bit of money and then, suddenly, they're out of the league. I've always tried to keep the mind-set that it could happen to me, and if it does, will I be financially prepared to deal with it? To me, what I *need* is a house, a car, and college funds for my kids. Everything else can be considered a luxury. Once I decided to treat myself to a Jaguar S-Type, but it just wasn't me so I got rid of it.

I just think that some people get too caught up in having more money when it's really a privilege to have any. I remember at the Pro Bowl, Bill Cowher would get the team in a huddle and lead us in a chant: "Don't mess with my money on three." I was thinking, "Who in the heck is this guy? Is he serious? I'm not saying that." I don't know if he was saying it because of the audience he had, but I thought it was stupid for a coach to use $17,500—the bonus for winning the game—as motivation. I represent myself in contract negotiations, and sometimes I get flack for not being a mercenary. The last contract I signed I got a $3.5 million bonus on a deal worth $8 million overall. And I got criticized for it. Think about that. I've negotiated a few deals with the Patriots and they've always put a number in front of me that's bearable. I know it could be more, but it's still all right. I guess you have to be comfortable in your own skin, knowing that someone else is making more money. Someone else makes more than I do? Congratulations. If I were greedy and sought more money elsewhere, I would have been a free-agent linebacker who'd had a stroke. Imagine finding work then.

At times it amazes me how far Tony, Natalia, and I have come since childhood. Tony is now a supervisor for a construction company in Las Vegas. Natalia is the big-timer of the family. She does hair and makeup for an agency in Los Angeles. She has worked with some A-list people: Matt Damon, Al Pacino, Colin Farrell, Ben Stiller, Dustin Hoffman, Ben Affleck, and Topher Grace. She's worked in Europe and all over the world. She is what you would call a self-made woman, and I'm really proud of her.

As for me, sometimes I sit back and think that I'm turning

into my father. I think the way I am now with my family is where he wanted to get to in life. At times, he was very bitter during those weekend visitations, and it seemed like he was always pleading his side of the story. But underneath it all I think he was broken up about being separated from my mom and us being separated as a family. He had to cram all of his ideas on parenting into the weekends that he had us. Sometimes he would sit us down for hours at a time at the kitchen table or in the living room with the TV off. He would talk to us about values, respect, being good to one another, and respecting the elderly. He was an old-school guy.

My father died in 2001, but I'm probably closer to him now than I was when he was alive. We had an uneven relationship when he was alive, but I hear him more now than I did when he was here. It was as if he died and my memory of some of the knowledge he tried to put on me got better. It hits me when I'm driving in the car with the boys and I'll say something that my father would have said.

I know that, ideally, he would have liked to have had some financial independence. He would have wanted to have a fallback plan just in case something unexpected happened. I had those thoughts when I was leaving the University of Arizona for the NFL. But I was thinking that the only things that could end my career would be some football-related injury or a lack of talent. Stroke, a word that you usually associate with grandmothers and grandfathers, never occurred to me. In many ways, my education was just beginning.

3

TEDY BRUSCHI, ORGANIZATIONAL TRAINEE

I was a lost man and I knew it. It was the end of February 2005, and as March approached, everything that had been a certainty for me before was in flux. I was officially a member of the Patriots, but it felt as if I didn't have a team or a job. I would hang around the house, seemingly in a perpetual holding pattern, wondering what the next day would bring.

I had a new life, with new characters being introduced all the time. Before, I could count on football to shape my calendar for me. I never had to wonder what to do next because all I had to do was look at the month and the answer was right there. Whether it was the off-season training program in March, mini-camp in June, or training camp in July, I always knew what to do and how to prepare for it. Suddenly, from my health to my life, I didn't feel that I could give anyone definitive answers about what was happening next.

In this new life, immediately following my release from the hospital, the late-February calendar called for daily home visits from a nurse named Debbie Reynolds. Debbie was there to regulate my intake of a blood thinner called Coumadin. She was as pleasant and attentive as any patient could want, but I honestly felt like I was seventy-five years old each time she arrived for her visits. I'm sure she sensed it, too.

"Oh, you're young," she would say in her thick New England accent. "All of my other patients are older."

I wasn't used to my body not being able to do what I told it. I would walk from room to room in my old house—the house wasn't big at all—and even those short walks would wear me out. I knew I needed surgery to repair the hole in my heart. I still couldn't drive because my vision was impaired. On top of that, I wasn't encouraged by the way I was moving; I was still dragging my left foot. As for the blood thinners, I was taking them to prevent any additional clotting.

If I had any routine early in my recovery, it was waiting for Debbie. She would walk through the door, with a scent of cigarettes on her clothes, simultaneously chatty and matter-of-fact; she talked a lot about her husband and son, yet she never wasted our time. She was focused on the fact that she was there to help me get in the right range for Coumadin. I learned that if my range was too high my blood would be too thin, and if it was too low it would be too thick. There was always a range number to report, and after a while I'd make a game out of what that number would be.

"I think I'm going to be a 1.2 today, Debbie," I'd say to her.

She'd check the numbers and say excitedly, "Look at that: you're right."

My pills were pink and oval-shaped, and in the beginning they were a milligram apiece. Some nights I would have to take 3.5 milligrams, and on others it would be 7.5. The number changed a lot the first week, but after I got regulated I switched to 5-milligram pills and didn't have to take as many. Taking the blood thinners made me understand why Terry Francona, the manager of the Boston Red Sox, often wears a red fleece during their games. You get cold easily, so I found myself wearing more clothes around the house.

I was worn down physically. In addition to the pills, I also had to take Fragmin, a drug that prevents clotting. When Dr. Greer first told me I had to take it, I said, "Okay, where are the pills?"

"There are no pills," he said. "You have to inject it."

"Needles don't scare me," I said. "No problem."

"Well, you have to take the shot in your stomach," he said.

And that's when I started asking for the pills again. My stomach? I wasn't excited about it, but I allowed Heidi to give me the shots in the beginning. I was queasy initially, but eventually I started giving myself the shots. Many times it looked as if there were polka dots the size of silver dollars on my stomach. They were big black bruises, and they were in so many places on my stomach that I had a hard time finding an open abdominal space that wasn't bruised. And if those weren't enough signs that I was far away from a football career, I was working with a therapist who was teaching me how to regain the strength in my body.

Every player thinks of life after football, but it's usually a distant vision that doesn't include rehab and therapy. You want it to be on your terms, at an age when you either feel that there is no more football left in you or you no longer have the desire to play. I still wanted to be there, but it wasn't an option that Heidi and I wasted our time discussing. Stroke had changed our lives, but at that point we still didn't understand it. We thought we were doing what we were supposed to do. There was no long family discussion about the pros and cons of playing because, frankly, we thought it was impossible.

It was early March 2005, well before the NFL draft and a couple weeks into free agency. I thought if I told the Patriots what I planned to do, they would have time to draft and sign some linebackers. I also realized there was a lot I didn't know about my contractual rights as I came to the end of my career. I am literally one in a thousand when it comes to self-representation. Most NFL players have agents who negotiate on their behalf, structure contracts, research league trends, and monitor all the small-print items. I was on my own, and that had always been fine for regular contract negotiations. My approach has always been fairly simple: I always listen to what the team has to say, and I never take it personally when they raise questions about my age or the durability of my knees. It's a negotiating tactic for all the executives I've hammered out deals with—Andy Wasynczuk, Jack Mula, and Scott Pioli—and I understand it. When I do deals, I'm not interested in reciting all the things I'll be able to do, because I believe they already know. Let's just cut out the nonsense and get to an agreement that's fair.

That philosophy has always worked for me, but everyone doesn't agree with it. Brad Blank, a Boston-based agent, is one of those people. Brad used to argue that I was taking below-market deals. Sometimes I'd listen to him, and sometimes he'd critique my negotiating and I'd simply give him a look; he would tell mutual friends of ours that I'd lock my jaw and seemingly stare right through him. Brad used to represent Chris Slade, one of my former teammates. After the stroke, I called Chris and asked him what he thought of Brad, a fast-talking man who grew up in the same Massachusetts town as the Kennedys (Hyannisport) and can probably work a room as well as any of them.

"Chris, can you vouch for this guy?" I asked.

"Tedy, I can definitely vouch for him," he answered.

That's when I decided to call Brad. I had several reasons for making the call. I wanted to know if the Patriots could take back anything from me. I had just signed a new contract and had three years remaining on it. I wasn't sure what was going to happen. I had seen some nasty contract disputes and player exits in Foxboro, from Lawyer Milloy to Ty Law to Drew Bledsoe to Deion Branch. Was that going to affect me? I knew my situation was different and anticipated that it might be handled differently from theirs, but I had to protect myself. I didn't want to be taken advantage of, and I didn't want anything to happen to what I'd already earned. I needed Brad to be a bit of a security blanket and give me information that I didn't have.

The first thing I asked for was an explanation of lawyer-client confidentiality. He explained that it meant he couldn't tell anyone what I said to him unless I waived the right.

"Well, listen," I said. "I want to hire you so you can help me understand everything I'm entitled to as a retired player. I've had a stroke, I have a hole in my heart, and I won't be able to play football again. You're my lawyer now, so everything I've just told you is confidential."

He said he'd do some research so he could figure out the best route to take from there. He also advised me to call the owner, Robert Kraft, and the head coach, Bill Belichick, tell them my plan to retire, and let them know that he was now my representative. It wasn't long before I took his advice.

Most of the time I was glad to be representing myself as an athlete and a businessman, but in this case I was relieved to have some separation. When I talked to Mr. Kraft, I didn't want an awkward business conversation to be shadowing us. He is the owner of a successful NFL franchise, one that is worth over $1 billion, so it would be natural for him to have thoughts about my retirement and its impact on his corporation. I wasn't interested in having that type of conversation with him. Brad could deal with him regarding the business concerns at another time, and I could focus on delivering the difficult news about my career.

I've always had good exchanges with Mr. Kraft on all topics, serious and silly. There have been times when we've talked about our wives, and he's shared some things that he went through early in his marriage with Myra. We have had lighthearted conversations about the best restaurants to go to in Boston and the best places to get sushi in Chestnut Hill, which is near his home. There have been times when he's walked through the locker room during moments when the players are having one of our meaningless debates about food. Once, before Thanksgiving, we were talking about making turkeys. Some guys in the room were passionately defending dark meat as the best, while others were celebrating the strengths of white meat. At that moment, we saw Mr. Kraft walking through the locker room. "Mr. Kraft," one of us said, "dark meat or white meat?" We paused, waited for his answer—he said dark meat—and then the couple dozen guys who agreed with him applauded and patted him on the back. I knew he was fun, a sincere fan, a good businessman, and a powerful owner.

I called him at home. He asked me how I was doing and I told him that I was feeling better. He said he was glad to hear it, and then I told him what I called to say. I remember that it was six-thirty or seven in the evening and I was sitting in our nursery. The only light that was on at the time was the dim one from the hallway. It was a quiet scene for what was going to be a brief and somber conversation. I was emotional, not in a teary kind of way, but it was a sadness—borderline guilt—that I had let him down. I don't know how you let someone down by having a stroke, but I was just disappointed to be ending my career that way. He was very supportive and understanding. I think, from his conversations with Brad, he knew what was coming. The talk with Mr. Kraft was difficult enough to have over the phone, but I can imagine it would have been much worse in person.

With that said, I felt that I had to meet with Bill Belichick face-to-face. I remember calling his assistant, Berj Najarian, and asking if Bill would be in town the next day. I was told that he would, so I scheduled an appointment to see him at 9 A.M. It was going to be an unusual trip to the stadium for my family. I can recall every minor detail about that morning. Heidi and I got the boys loaded into the minivan, she took the wheel, and I sat in the middle row flanked by my sons. We began to make the twelve-minute trip to Gillette Stadium, and as we made that familiar drive, I came up with a plan of what I'd do once we arrived. I was going to head to the empty locker room first, clean out my things, and then leave them near the players' entrance to the stadium. That way, I could make a quick and clean escape out of Bill's office if I needed to. As Heidi parked in the players' parking lot, she asked me if I wanted her and the boys to walk in with me. I told her that this was something I needed to do alone, so they waited outside as I approached the door.

I was unemotional as I went to the locker room, stared at the cherrywood stall with "54" above it, and removed everything I needed. Then it was time for the tough part. I made my way toward Bill's office, passing meeting rooms and assistant coaches' offices on the way. Whether the stadium here was called Foxboro or Gillette, it had been my professional home since I left Arizona. Bill wasn't my first head coach in the league, but he had taught me a lot and we had been to four Super Bowls together, winning three of them. I had several thoughts before I walked into his office.

Our relationship has always been a good one. My first couple years around him, I wanted to see more emotion from him. I used to think, "Come on, man. Give me a shoulder bump or something!" But I learned what kind of person he is. He genuinely cares about people—and cares about me—but he shows it in a different way. Whereas other people came to see me when I was in the hospital, he didn't visit; he called. He checked on how I was doing and told me if there was anything I needed, the team was there for me.

I had no idea what he would say or how I would respond as I walked into his office. He sat at his desk, surrounded by reminders of our success. He didn't know it, but if he had looked out of the large window behind him, he would have seen a minivan holding my wife and sons. They were in there watching a DVD, waiting for me to emerge from this meeting. It was the first time I had seen Bill since the stroke, and soon I would tell him that my name would never again be on the team depth chart.

We started with small talk. I told him I was getting better, although my sight was still bad. I told him the left side of my body was gradually getting stronger and that I hoped my rehab would bring even more rapid improvement. "But," I said, "what I really came here to tell you—although the season is a long way away—is that I'm not going to be here for you next year. I'm going to retire."

I was able to get the words out, but I was aching inside. Talking to Mr. Kraft over the phone was tough, but he was at his house and I was at mine. This seemed more real and more final because it was at the stadium. I had been in Bill's office many times to talk about something related to the game. I never imagined I would be sitting across from him having a retirement conversation. He listened to what I had to say, and then he surprised me. He said something that I couldn't see at the time but I find extremely intelligent now. While a lot of people— including me at times—would like to see Bill be more outwardly emotional, keeping emotions out of things benefits the way he thinks. Other people's minds can be racing, but Bill's is calm. He slows things down and thinks logically.

"Well, have you ever thought of just taking the year off like Mark Fields did?"

I heard the question clearly, but it didn't sink in for me.

Fields, also a linebacker, didn't play in 2003 for the Carolina Panthers because he was diagnosed with Hodgkin's disease. I didn't think our situations were similar and I still wasn't fully educated about stroke. Bill had the right idea and asked a perfectly valid question, but I hadn't gone to the stadium that day to entertain new questions. I knew what I had to do and say.

"No, there's not going to be a difference between this year and next year," I said. "I still have to deal with this heart procedure, and I can barely walk. The year off is not going to help me. I've made up my mind. I'm retiring."

I could feel it coming then. I was emotional over what I was saying and what I was doing. I hated the feeling of letting the team down. I took Tom Brady seriously when he talked of winning three Super Bowls in a row. I wanted to win again with the group of players we had, players I respected and loved. Although I had sat at my kitchen table and mentioned the word "retirement" to my wife and family, I had never hinted at it with my coaches and teammates. Whenever anyone called or visited, they would ask how I was doing. Football never came into the conversation. I think there was a silent understanding that I wouldn't be playing anymore. But I was there that day, sitting across from Bill, verbalizing everything that I had only thought before.

Bill wished me the best and told me, just as he had during our conversation at the hospital, that if there was anything I needed the team would be there for me. I mentioned that I would still be around the stadium rehabbing with a therapist from Spaulding Rehabilitation Hospital. I asked if that would be okay.

"Absolutely, Tedy," he said. "You'll always be welcome around here."

Hearing that phrase from Bill got to me. That's something you say to former players, and that's what I was. I started to break down, but I shook his hand as best I could. I left the office, which is the first one players see when they walk into the stadium. My bags were already by the door, so I picked them up and slowly walked toward the parking lot. During the season, the same parking lot is filled with players' and coaches' cars. For road games, the parking lot is lined with several chartered buses, idling before they take us to the airport in Providence. On those days, there is a buzz to the place. But on the March morning I walked out of the stadium with my things, the lot was quiet and nearly vacant. Heidi has seen me in every emotional state imaginable, so she knew I was struggling long before I returned to the minivan. We hugged when I got there, and as she drove, I cried on the way home. I remember TJ asking, "What's wrong, Daddy?" And I just said to him, "Daddy's just a little sad, buddy. Just a little sad."

I remember passing the End Zone Motor Inn, the Lafayette House Restaurant, and all the places I'd driven by for years. I kept shaking my head because I was having a hard time grasping that it was over so suddenly. I thought of how I had adopted New England and how the region adopted me as well. It's a blue-collar region with hardworking families, so that's one of the obvious reasons that I fell in love with it. I arrived in New England and sort of grew in front of everyone's eyes. I thought of how New Englanders have seen me progress, slowly, as a player before them. It's not like I got to town and started ballin' out and they asked, "Where did this great player come from?" It was a process. They saw me get better and they heard me honestly talk about the things that were on my mind. They've heard me speak about some of the problems I've had with drinking, and they know that family is as important to me as it is to them. In a way, my stroke and my retirement would be another way for the residents of the region to relate to me. My stroke is someone else's cancer. It's someone else going through hard times, or someone else losing a loved one. I thought of my career as we drove away, and it was clear that it was not just a normal football career. It was a development of my life as well.

I had talked with Mr. Kraft and Bill, so now it was time to come up with the next phase of my life. I wasn't sure what I was going to do because I was still passionate about one career: pro football. It was taken away overnight, and I hadn't seriously planned for anything else. Because of my financial approach, money wasn't an issue. We had planned—before the stroke—to sell the house on Red Oak Road and move to a new home a couple miles away that was already paid for. The only unanswered question was: what was I going to do? Brad would eventually hear from several people with job proposals. NBC called him and asked if I would be open to doing studio work during football season. The NFL Network called him and said it had a job for me. Brad also began to explore possibilities with local television work. But all of those were either secondary or peripheral options. For a while, all of his energy was directed toward working out a deal with Mr. Kraft.

It really did feel like I was starting over. It had been years since someone had gone to the Patriots and spoken on my behalf. But I felt that Brad had a good relationship with the organization, and he would think of things that I wouldn't know to bring up. I have a great relationship with Brad now, but we did have a major rough spot in the first couple of months that he started working for me. It was so rough that for a few hours I actually fired him. The problem arose when Brad made a brief comment about my future plans to a local reporter. I saw Brad's quote in the paper and became incensed that he would comment at all to anyone about what I was doing or what I planned to do. Brad called me at home to explain himself, but it was hard for me to listen to him. At the time, I didn't want any aspect of my story reported in the media, and if I did want the story told, I was confident that I could tell it myself.

I got so angry with Brad that at one point he said, "Tedy, if you're not satisfied with the representation I'm giving you, maybe you should look somewhere else." I paused for a couple seconds and realized that Brad didn't know me as well as he might have thought. "Okay," I said, "you're fired." Brad called back and talked with Heidi, who was able to make him understand why I was so worked up. After some cooling off, I was able to talk to Brad again, and he was once again my representative. Even if I had been an expert on the bylaws in contracts, I had other things to concentrate on, so I needed Brad to handle contractual business. I was scheduled for the heart procedure on March 15, and I would have to resume my rehab after that.

I left all the business conversations with Mr. Kraft in Brad's hands and waited for him to come to me with any news. Much later, he told me about the first in-person conversation they had regarding me. It was at Mr. Kraft's Brookline home, a home members of the team know well because our Super Bowl ring ceremony had taken place there the previous June. Mr. Kraft and Brad are Jewish, so they both talked about the importance of the Yiddish word "mensch." If you call someone a mensch, you're complimenting his character and integrity. Brad mentioned the word because he wanted to make the point to Mr. Kraft that he could solidify his reputation as one of the great mensches in the area if he honored my contract.

I guess one of the advantages of representing yourself is that you get to know the people you work for in a way completely different from that of most agents and players. Brad had tough negotiations with Mr. Kraft in the past, but I'd never experienced that. Then again, I'd never had to have a touchy conversation with the owner of the team about honoring my contract following a stroke. Brad consulted the NFL Players' Association in case things got messy.

Mr. Kraft was told that my agent's mandate was to get the organization to honor the remaining three years on the deal. When former Patriots running back Robert Edwards suffered what appeared to be a career-ending leg injury in 1999, the team paid him when it didn't have to. But when Mr. Kraft asked the other owners for some relief on the salary cap in the Edwards case, he didn't get it. He considered that to be one of his coming-of-age moments as an owner, and he brought that up in the meeting with Brad. He also said that a retired player with "dead money" on the salary cap would truly be restrictive to the team.

"All right, mensch to mensch," Mr. Kraft said. "What does Tedy need? Because I have an idea."

"I think we need to find a way to take care of Tedy," Brad replied.

"Well, what do you think of the idea of him working here?" Mr. Kraft said.

Brad told him that it was a good idea. Coaching was out, but I would be given a title: Tedy Bruschi, organizational trainee. The plan was for me to do a hybrid of marketing, sales, television, and corporate affairs jobs. It would involve everything outside of football operations. Mr. Kraft was indeed a mensch: it was a five-year contract with an extremely generous salary. There were just a couple of snags that needed to be cleaned up. One potential problem was something Mr. Kraft would have to take care of at the owners' meetings in Hawaii: possible cap evasion. (Some teams try giving extra money to their players by creating bogus jobs. This is a clear violation of the salary cap.) The other owners would have to be convinced that Mr. Kraft wasn't giving me a lucrative job to do nothing. I was assured that cap evasion would be a nonissue league-wide.

Everything appeared to be set. At home, Heidi was ecstatic. She even brought out our special red dinner plate for the occasion. The plate was a gift to us, and we use a permanent marker to write the date and occasion on the bottom of it. So on the bottom of the celebratory plate, Heidi wrote, "March 9th—Tedy ends his career. March 30th—Tedy accepts position with the Patriots." It was a sad way to end a career, yes, but we were excited to be moving on to something that would challenge me and allow me to be the husband and father I wanted to be.

Brad and the Patriots lawyers drafted a document that outlined my job responsibilities. I remember it being approved pretty quickly, and then going through a series of sectional rewrites and corrections. Brad came to my house several times and we went over the contract, paragraph by paragraph. After looking at the deal a few times, a couple of things hit me. One was that I just couldn't bring myself to participate in any of the television stuff during training camp. The thought of doing TV—as a panelist or analyst—while my teammates played football hurt me. It was too soon for me. A lot of those guys were like family members to me, and I couldn't imagine sitting in a booth analyzing them. And then there was the issue of the booth itself: did I belong there? I was retired, yet in my heart I was still a football player; I was not a former player explaining the game in layman's terms on TV. If I was that guy, I didn't feel like it. It was a confusing time for me. I was going back and forth between the generosity of Mr. Kraft and the whispers in my heart: *You're not done yet, are you? Are you ready for this to be the next phase of your life?*

I wasn't going to be able to handle doing anything in training camp or the preseason. We finally took the TV aspect out of the contract until year two of the five-year deal.

If you looked at all aspects of the contract, it was a sweet deal. It allowed me to stay in New England with the Patriots, gracefully walk away from the game, and make a good salary. I had plenty of time to analyze the contract because, after the final round of revisions, I asked Brad if I could keep the documents at my house and study them one last time. I told him that he could come by the house the following weekend to pick up the signed papers. I'm not a procrastinator, but something kept me from signing my name. After a few days, Brad called and asked the best time for him to retrieve the contract.

"This weekend is no good," I told him. "How about next week?"

I was stalling and Brad could sense it. There was a wonderful deal on the table, but I wasn't moving with any urgency to accept it. After a couple more delays, I finally told Brad that I wasn't going to sign it. I was a signature away from a completely different football life, and then the deal was on the cutting-room floor. I appreciated the effort, creativity, and generosity that went into the agreement, but it didn't feel natural to me.

Not many things felt natural to me at that time. It didn't have as much to do with my body as it did my mind. My body, as weak as it was, still healed faster than my psyche. I wasn't unlike any other person who had a stroke. It physically knocks you on your butt, and it can also mess with your mind. In the early stages of my rehab, I was more focused on getting my body back to normal, even though I was dealing with a lot of confusion and uncertainty. The first three months of 2005 had been packed with several dramatic moments, positive and otherwise. My youngest son was born in January, and we bought a new house; the Patriots won the Super Bowl in February, I played in the Pro Bowl, and I had a stroke. I retired in March, had a flap closed in my heart, and thought about working for the team.

I still hadn't spoken publicly, and the people of New England had a lot of questions about what I was going to do next. I wasn't sure myself. The fans and some members of the media were sincerely concerned about how I was doing, but for some in the media it was a race to see who could get the story first. Less than twenty-four hours after I had the stroke, the friends who were staying at our house said that reporters were knocking on the door. Another time I was home and getting ready to play outside with TJ when a Boston TV reporter, Phil Lipof, showed up with a Channel 7 cameraman. I made eye contact with Lipof, and I swear I could see the shame on his face. He really struggled to look me in the eyes for a few seconds. I think he knew what he was doing was in poor taste, but it seemed as if he made the decision that getting the story was more important than my family's privacy. I saw Lipof and his cameraman—who was scrambling to get a clear shot of me—and told TJ that we would go outside another day.

It got to the point where we had to have security on our street to keep the media away. I knew I would eventually speak with reporters. I thought I was ready a few times, and once I talked with the Patriots about coordinating a pool interview with a reporter named Gary Gillis. I would tell him everything, and then the interview would be distributed for all media outlets to use. The plan was in place but, once again, I wasn't in the right state of mind to go through with a plan that had been carefully discussed. It was hard for me to articulate emotions for other people to understand when I still had to sort through them for myself. The Patriots were getting dozens of interview requests from the national and local media, and Brad was getting about fifteen requests per week. After a while, it seemed like my answer to everything was a nonnegotiable "No."

I was keeping a lot of feelings inside, so even some of my closest teammates didn't know how I felt. When I'm on the field,

I have to be decisive as a middle linebacker. I have to be decisive in my defensive calls so my teammates know what we're doing. But away from the field I surprised myself at how indecisive I was. I didn't feel like a part of the team anymore, even though I hadn't told any player about my retirement. I still felt like a man whom people pitied, and when I got that vibe it would make me sink deeper into my hole.

During that time, my instinct was to withdraw from the crowd. Sometimes I felt like I wanted to disappear. So, initially, I decided to pass on the Patriots' April trip to the White House to celebrate the Super Bowl win. And when the Red Sox called about throwing out the first pitch at their home opener—celebrating their first World Series title in eighty-six years—I said no to that request, too. Fortunately for me, I couldn't disappear at home. Heidi knew I was thinking about skipping the White House trip, and she told me I had to go. She said the same thing about throwing out the first pitch at Fenway Park.

"It's an honor to do both things," she said. "Being with all the guys at the White House will be fun, and you have a chance to be on the field the same day the Red Sox get their rings. I don't want you to have any regrets. You have to do these things."

She was right, so I changed my mind again.

4

BODY AND SOUL

This sounds like the retelling of a dream, but it actually happened: on a sunny April afternoon in Boston, I stood near Fenway Park's famous left-field wall, the 37-foot-high Green Monster, and threw baseballs with Bill Russell, Bobby Orr, and my teammate Richard Seymour. The four of us talked about golf, winning championships, and raising children. We all laughed whenever Russell did, because his distinct cackle leaves you with no other choice. We joked about our throws and how we didn't want to embarrass ourselves when we took the field in front of a sellout crowd. On a day when the Red Sox might be celebrating their first World Series title since 1918, the four of us had been selected to simultaneously throw out the ceremonial first pitch.

Heidi couldn't have said it better; it was an honor for me to be there. Russell and Orr are New England sports icons, Hall of Famers, and two of the best players in NBA and NHL history. They also tell great stories. Before we threw our pitches, we sat in a holding room with our wives, girlfriends, and, in some cases, children. The room was stocked with sandwiches and drinks. All of us sat around a table, eating and being captivated by Russell's stories. He got Heidi's attention when he told a story about his daughter, Karen, being the first ballgirl in the NBA. The Celtics needed someone to do the job in the 1960s and were looking for a boy. Karen convinced her father that she and a friend were just as capable as any teenage boys.

"I'm glad that you weren't a chauvinist," Heidi said when she heard the story.

"Oh, no," Russell replied. "I had no choice. My daughter wouldn't let me."

He laughed and we laughed with him. It would have been enough for me to sit and listen to their stories, but I also got a chance to talk to Carl Yastrzemski, another Hall of Famer, and Dwight Evans. They told me they were praying for me and offered their support. After a lot of laughs and conversation, it was time to take the field. Soon we would walk across an outfield that looked like soft green carpet.

Fenway is the oldest park in Major League Baseball, but it looked great that day. There was a huge American flag draping the wall, and the four of us stood behind it waiting to be introduced. I was in awe. I obviously hadn't been feeling like myself for several weeks and I didn't think I was ready to be in front of thousands of fans. But some of that uncertainty went away when my name was announced, last of the four, followed by an ovation that shook me. I couldn't believe how loud it was. As we all started walking together, I heard thousands of people chanting, "Ted-y, Ted-y, Ted-y . . ." And there I was walking with one of

my teammates alongside Bill Russell and Bobby Orr. I was flab-
bergasted. I had always been amazed by Orr, from the way he
played to the greatness of his golf game to his youthful looks (he
had recently turned fifty-seven). But he glanced at me as we
walked as if to say, "Can you believe this?" Russell had spoken
to our team after our first Super Bowl win, but my admiration
for him went all the way back to my childhood. He went to
college in San Francisco, and I grew up there as an accidental
Celtics fan. My older brother, Tony, was always a fan of the
Philadelphia 76ers. I didn't want to take Tony's team, so one day
I asked him whom I should root for. "Root for Boston," he said.
"They're pretty good, too." That's when I started to follow all
things Celtics. I just felt so fortunate to be on the field with the
ultimate basketball champion, being recognized by the fans and
taking part in Red Sox history.

The Red Sox wanted the four of us to be representatives of
Boston's professional sports teams. So Seymour wore a Patriots
jersey, Russell had on a Celtics jacket, Orr sported his familiar
number 4 Bruins sweater, and I had on a number 47 Red Sox
jersey. I wore it as a sign of respect for Terry Francona, a fellow
University of Arizona alum and the manager of the Red Sox.
Francona had had a heart scare one week earlier in Yankee
Stadium when he left the park a few hours before the game and
checked into a hospital. He complained of tightness in his chest
and was held overnight, but everything checked out okay. He
knew I was going to be at Fenway for the opener, but he didn't
know I would be wearing his jersey. He got a little choked up
when he saw the red 47 on my back, and by the time he reached
me on the mound he was teary-eyed. So was I. He talked to me

the way a lot of old Italians do: he cupped the back of my head with his hand and looked me in the eyes.

"I've been praying for you and thinking about your situation so much," he said. "You don't know how much I care about you, Tedy."

I wished him well, and he insisted that he catch the ball I was going to throw. I was wearing white sneakers with no traction. I kept thinking that I couldn't slip, and not just because it would be embarrassing. I felt if I slipped it would start a new round of speculation and commentary about the stroke. Throwing a bad first pitch would raise questions, too. If Seymour, Russell, and Orr happened to throw poorly, it would be interpreted a lot differently than if I did.

When I came out of the wall with the Boston legends, I consciously overemphasized my normal walk. You could even say I was strutting, just to be careful. By the time we threw our pitches, I was a lot more relaxed than I had been going in. Being at Fenway was a break from the stress that Heidi and I had been experiencing for weeks. There was an incredible display of affection from the fans, and being there prevented me from continuing to hide at home. There was no pity party from anyone, and that made me feel better.

I threw a high-arcing ball to Francona, and it reached him easily. All of us were satisfied with our throws, including Russell, who bounced his well short of the plate. When he saw where his pitch landed, he gave a good-natured laugh.

I went home feeling great that day. I watched all the coverage on the news and read the paper the next morning. There were pictures and an article that Heidi and I read with smiles on our faces. The line that got our attention was the one that read, "Bruschi walked with a noticeable limp." And that was probably the first time in a while that Heidi and I laughed. There was no question that a strut was going on, but there was no limp. That it was written was funny to us.

In early April, I felt that laughing at anything was a positive for me. As many stroke survivors can tell you, there can be marked emotional swings from day to day, and I wasn't any different. Getting to Fenway was one of the good days. But there were other times when I focused on the changes in my life. I had the PFO, or patent foramen ovale, repaired on March 15. It's a heart condition present in 30 percent of the population. My middle son, Rex, had a PFO when he was born, but when he was checked six months later the small hole had closed. My PFO had allowed a blood clot to form and reach my brain, a sequence that led to the stroke.

The doctor who performed the surgery was Igor Palacios, and he inserted a thin device into my femoral artery—which is near the groin—and maneuvered it until it reached my heart. The device was as thin as pencil lead when it traveled through my body. When it was released, it expanded to the size of a nickel. It rested on my heart, and eventually tissue healed over it and made it a permanent part of my heart. I'm talking about it calmly now, but I was angry just minutes before the surgery. There was a research consent form I was asked to sign because the doctors wanted to continue to study those who had the device. I felt like a guinea pig.

"I shouldn't be doing this," I said to Heidi. "Why am I letting them put something in me? I really shouldn't be doing this."

I knew the answer to my own question. I was letting them do it because I didn't like the alternatives: I would either have open-heart surgery or be put on blood thinners for the rest of my life. We felt that the procedure, which had been in use for ten years, was the best option. We knew the risks; they were stated plainly and clearly on the consent form: "There is no guarantee that this procedure will benefit you. However, successfully placed closure of the defect may cancel the need for cardiac surgery and other complications."

I had a persistent thought just before surgery: What if this doesn't work?

The procedure took place about three and a half weeks before the baseball game. So while I was able to throw a baseball and talk with legendary Boston sports figures, I was not allowed to pick up my own sons.

One of the postprocedure rules was that I couldn't bear down or do any type of straining for six weeks. Dr. Palacios explained that, early on, any type of bearing down would push blood through the device and prevent tissue from healing over it. It was tough, because I'm very physical with TJ and Rex. They jump on me and push me down and jump off the couches, all kinds of stuff. I like to tackle them and give them hugs. It's sort of my way of being affectionate with them, too. Dante was two and a half months old on March 15, and I missed a stage of being able to pick him up and carry him and walk him around. It was something that was eating me up. It hurt inside because that's what fathers do. At that age, your dad will always pick you up and give you a hug, right? I couldn't, and I felt a little bit less as a father.

TJ and Rex would ask me to pick them up often. Normally, it's not unusual for me to give them piggybacks or carry them up the stairs as they're going to bed. They like to get on my back and give a mock squeeze, like they're choking me, until I drop them on the couch. They'd say, "Daddy, pick me up," and I'd just tell them, "I can't." I tried to follow Dr. Palacios's directions to the letter, but I did cheat twice. Once I lifted Dante onto a swing, I think it was week five or six, and the other time I carried TJ and Rex upstairs so I could tuck them in at bedtime.

Some days I had no problem with what my life had become, and other days I felt sorry for myself. Two days after going to Fenway, I started to look at my situation differently. I was going to make that trip to the White House with several teammates and coaches on April 13. It was going to be my third Washington visit in four years, but there would be a couple of different twists this time. My first obstacle was going to be getting over my newfound fear of flying. I hadn't been on a plane since coming back from Hawaii, when the blood clot that caused the stroke may have formed. I talked with Dr. Greer about the ninety-minute flight to Washington and he told me I'd be fine. I was, but I was a little bit of a basket case on the way there. I was on Mr. Kraft's private jet, and of all the features on it, I can tell you most about the bathroom. I spent most of the flight in there, doing stretches, touching my toes, and lifting my legs. It's a small bathroom, but I would sit down in there and do a number of exercises. I don't think all of that was necessary for such a short flight, but I was nervous.

I was among a group of players that made an important stop before going to the White House. We went to Walter Reed Army

Hospital so we could visit the troops home from the war. Shortly after arriving at the hospital that day, I remember talking to a soldier who had been injured and then later had a stroke. His was a lot worse than mine. He was really disoriented. I tried to tell him my story, too, but he wasn't there yet. And that's when I realized how blessed I was. Seeing him and his stroke and other soldiers who had lost limbs brought some things into focus for me.

These men were excited to see us. Some of them were showing us their wounds, and in some cases the wounds were really holes. You could see into one soldier's rib cage, and he gave the details of where he was blasted from stepping on a landmine. They weren't ashamed. Some of them were amputees and they said, "I can't wait to get back out there." For them, "out there" wasn't out of the hospital to be with other civilians. "Out there" was back to war. It was incredible to see the fight they had in them, even though they were injured. One guy said, "I lost my arm but they say I can go back." I was just astounded at the courage these warriors were showing. I had a lot of things going on in my mind, and seeing them helped me tremendously. It was my life, my stroke, and my own adversity that I had to overcome, but my problems felt much less significant when compared to theirs. Their attitude about coming back from whatever injury they had was inspiring to me.

We stayed at the hospital for a couple of hours, visiting different floors and the rehab room. We had the three Super Bowl trophies and took them all over the hospital. The soldiers got something out of seeing us, but I'm sure the players in my group would agree that we got much more out of seeing them.

When we went to the White House, President Bush had a surprise for me. I wasn't expecting anything as I stood there in my navy suit and red tie. But as he gave his speech about our team, he turned and acknowledged me. He said he was happy that I had made the trip and that he was impressed with the courage I had shown on the field and off. And just think: Heidi had to convince me to go to Washington. The senators from Massachusetts, John Kerry and Ted Kennedy, also had comments for me. I was impressed that both of them went out of their way to introduce themselves and ask how I was doing. It was an educational trip by any definition. The visit to Fenway was good for my spirits and my soul, while going to Washington inspired me and also helped me understand the resiliency of the body. There was no bitterness from those soldiers who had been injured at war. They were passionate about fighting, even if it meant they would have to do it with one leg or one arm.

It seemed that for two months I had been constantly thinking about and getting an education on the body. I had been introduced to a lot of new medical terms and been cared for by brilliant doctors and therapists. The challenge for me, post-stroke and post-procedure, was to restore my body through rehab. A Marine's daughter, a woman named Anne McCarthy Jacobson, was assigned to help me do that.

Anne is a highly regarded physical therapist at Spaulding Rehabilitation Hospital in Boston. She specializes in neurologic and complex medical disorders. She has a good sense of humor, so she sometimes catches herself rhapsodizing about terminology, and calls herself a "neural geek." She is a pro football fan and a follower of the Patriots, but when she met me, I didn't resemble anything close to the linebacker she was used to seeing. She said she could immediately tell that I had something called left homonymous hemianopia. Yes, it's as scary as it sounds and looks, and for me it meant that I couldn't see to the left out of either eye. When I looked to the left there was either blackness or blurriness, and the odds were against me returning to normal: 60 percent of people who experience the total loss that I did will not have their vision return to 100 percent.

I started working with Anne the last week in February. We met three times a week for about ninety minutes at a time. The media knew I was doing rehab with Spaulding, but everyone assumed it was in Boston. Actually all of the sessions took place thirty miles away in Foxboro at Gillette Stadium. Anne took my privacy very seriously. I didn't ask her to be protective, but she still insisted on never writing my name on a piece of paper following our sessions. She was aware of the hyper media coverage and she wanted to be sure that something innocent—such as a sheet of paper containing my name and progression of exercises—didn't fall into the wrong hands and create a media exclusive. She used to joke that even if she got arrested and had her car confiscated, there wouldn't be anything in the vehicle with my name on it. The code of the Marines, integrity and honor, was something that she found relevant. I appreciated how careful she was and quickly grew to trust her.

From the start, Anne knew that I wasn't supposed to do any high-energy exercises, and I was humbled when I discovered what "high energy" was for me. Most well-conditioned athletes have to do a lot to get their heart rates over 100 beats per minute because they're in such good shape. It didn't take much for me, and when I reached 100 I had to stop. I was doing what I would usually consider remedial things, focused on coordination and balance. I had balance beams and I was supposed to do sidesteps on them. Every time I tried to walk sideways, I'd fall. If I tried to walk on the balance beam without my toes or heels touching the beam, I had problems. My entire left side was weak, and not just my arm and leg. I had lost a lot of strength in my hip extensors and glutes, muscles that are responsible for a power push or a quick burst.

It didn't take me long to understand what Anne was talking about when she mentioned the vestibular, or balance, system in the brain. Many of us take it for granted, but eyesight is very much connected to balance. In the early stages of rehab, with my vision slowly returning, I had trouble when Anne had me stand in front of her on a wooden balance board. I held on to her shoulders and she held my forearms. Whenever she removed her hands, I struggled and had to reach for her to avoid falling. There were tests to see what kind of balance reaction I had, and the results weren't uplifting; I couldn't balance at all without Anne's support.

Since the rehab took place at the stadium, I was close to football and yet far from it, too. There isn't a reasonably conditioned NFL player who would have found any of my early exercises challenging. Jim Whalen, the Patriots' head trainer, has seen many players do much more grueling things as they rehab from various pulls, tears, breaks, and sprains. He must have been shocked at how weak and uncoordinated I was when I did some of my workouts with Anne. But as frustrating as some of my balance issues were, they did provide good lessons on perspective. Anne is used to working with patients who have multiple sclerosis and amyotrophic lateral sclerosis, otherwise known as Lou Gehrig's disease. She said there are times when it takes her thirty minutes to get someone to roll over or thirty minutes to get them to sit up. So when I judged myself in an NFL context, I was doing horribly. But for a thirty-one-year-old stroke survivor trying to regain coordination, I was doing all right.

Some of the exercises became easier after the PFO procedure. My vision got better, which in turn made my balance and coordination better. With the PFO repaired, I began to gradually increase my exercise level. I started doing "gazelle leaps," or jumps from area to area. I did exercises where I raised myself up off my toes, which I simply couldn't do when I first tried. The problem was that I couldn't get my left heel off the ground. But I knew I was getting stronger. If I failed at a toe push-up on a Thursday, I'd succeed on the following Tuesday when I saw Anne. To test my dual-task ability, she'd have me stand on the balance board—on one foot—and actually recite multiplication tables. I would get frustrated on the days when I couldn't do it, but I liked the ideas behind everything I was being asked to do. I was being pushed.

Sometimes the pushing was literal. There were times I was told, "Twist your trunk." That is, I would twist as I put one hand on my shoulder and the other on my butt. Ideally, I'd be standing on my toes. From there, Anne would try to twist me more and I was supposed to resist. "Don't let me push you over," she would shout. "Fight me. Stay up on your toes." Many times I would be able to maintain resistance in my upper body, but I couldn't do it while standing on my toes. Then one day I did, without realizing it, and I saw Anne smiling.

"What?" I said.

"You're making my day," she answered. "This is going to be a great day."

I always appreciated Anne's perspective and honesty. She kept detailed notes, so whenever I'd become frustrated over an exercise that I couldn't do, she would remind me of how dramatic my improvement was since the previous session. "Well, look at it this way, Tedy: you couldn't do any of this at all last Tuesday," she would say. "You've made progress in just a couple days." But she didn't always tell me what I wanted to hear, and she wasn't condescending. If I didn't do an exercise the way she envisioned, she would say, "That was really great how you did that, but this time I want you to do it like this . . ."

My improvement started to become noticeable roughly at the same time as the NFL draft, which took place in late April. The Patriots had already signed two veteran linebackers, Monty Beisel and Chad Brown, and drafted a linebacker out of UNLV, a kid named Ryan Claridge. They were preparing to move on, and so was I.

Or was I?

Retirement, in my mind, was the logical thing to do in late February and early March. I had been struck by something that I had little knowledge of, and everything I did know pointed to no more football. There were some commonsense things that ruled it out, too. For example, I was still taking blood thinners in late April. There is no way that a doctor would allow a patient on blood thinners to take the field. Anne was concerned about me simply bumping my head when I was on Coumadin, because you bruise a lot easier when you're on a blood thinner. I couldn't fathom myself, taking Coumadin, returning to the most violent pro sport in America. But football did cross my mind as I started to recover.

I mentioned earlier that I have always been an impatient person, someone who would prefer to see results in twenty-four hours or less. I was even that way after having my heart procedure. For some reason, I didn't listen well enough when Dr. Palacios told me about the process of the tissue healing over the device. Obviously healing takes time, but I remember being angry with him and others when they did a "bubble" study during the echocardiogram *the day after* my surgery. The idea is to create tiny bubbles from saline water and then inject them into a vein. Doctors then watch the echo to see if they can find bubbles passing between the upper chambers of the heart, a scenario that would signify the presence of a PFO. Of course there were going to be bubbles the next day. I just remember thinking that the procedure didn't work—they had told me it would—and that my next option would be open-heart surgery. I don't recommend doing this to your doctors, but I looked at them like I was going to tackle them when they told me there were some bubbles passing through. It was crazy. It was as if I thought there would be surgery one day and the next day everything would be normal.

Later, I apologized to them profusely for my reaction. My lessons, though, were starting to repeat themselves. Whether it was the stroke, the heart procedure, rehab, or what I should do next, the themes were always the same. Wait. Be patient. Let things run their natural course. I had never been good in those areas. Before the stroke, my nature was always to see an issue and attack it for what it was that day, rarely considering what it might become in a week, a month, or even a year.

That's why I made such a quick decision on retirement. When I went home from the hospital in February, I did believe that I would return to normal. But to me that kind of normal was holding my kids and playing with them, and being a good husband to Heidi. I didn't include football in my future.

Then I started to, and Anne could sense it. I asked her in March, after I was retired, if she thought I could play again. I wasn't thinking of playing at that time, but I wanted to hear what she had to say. Anne said that she understood why I was asking the question and she thought it was appropriate, but she wasn't able to answer at that stage of my rehab. She began to get a better idea when I was finally allowed to start a running program. I was training like a football player, doing high-speed, or anaerobic, training on a treadmill. I would run all-out on a treadmill for twenty seconds, jump off and rest for twenty seconds, and then jump on again to repeat the process. It's a good way to simulate the stops and starts between plays in a game. I could feel myself changing as we headed into May. I knew I wasn't fooling myself. I knew I was getting to the point when I wouldn't have to work with Anne anymore. The key phrase with her was "neurological deficits," and I was reaching the point where I had none. I felt the best I had in months.

Of course, there was a major flaw in my thoughts about considering football again, which was that I was keeping those thoughts to myself. As far as Heidi knew, the two of us were still in sync. When I left for the stadium, I was going to rehab so I could have some use of the weakened left side of my body. She knew I wanted to retire with a good state of mind, that I wanted to be strong enough to, literally, walk away from the game. She knew that I had begun dropping hints to some of my teammates about not being there for them in 2006. I told Tom Brady that during one of our conversations, and I remember saying something similar to Rosevelt Colvin when he came to my house. Roman Phifer, Troy Brown, Joe Andruzzi, Ty Law, Mike Vrabel, Rodney Harrison, and Willie McGinest all checked up on me. I told them all that the Patriots might have to look for someone new to fill my role because I couldn't make any promises. (I also referred to Willie as "Dr. McGinest" in a text message once. In a conversation with the NFL Network, he had let it slip that I was having surgery to repair the PFO. I saw what he said on TV and sent him a short text: "Dr. McGinest, how am I doing now?" He said he was sorry for letting the information get out, but I really didn't mind because it was coming from Willie; he is one of those players who unquestionably gets the respect of anyone who comes into contact with him.) But I was still having bouts of indecisiveness, so some days I was there with Heidi about letting go of football. On other days, when the workouts started to become easy, I started to think about coming back. I was on an unpredictable emotional swing until one night in April when I had a raw conversation with my brother.

Tony is three years older than I am, but we could be twins at this point in our lives. We are similar people, the major difference being that he's a little brasher than I am. He knows how to talk to me, and I know how to get through to him. So he listened to me speak about how fragile I was emotionally and how

I was coping with being a young man who had a stroke and a heart procedure. He could hear my sadness over a football career that ended abruptly. I spoke of a lot of things that night, and I would have said even more if Tony hadn't interrupted me.

"You know what I think?" he said.

"What?"

"Man," Tony said with confidence, "I think you can play."

"You think I can play?"

"Ted, your heart's good. You can play. They can't stop you, man. They can't stop you."

It's funny to think about my brother saying those things, because he was just speaking from the gut. He doesn't have any medical expertise, and he really had no idea what I was supposed to be doing. But I needed to hear what he had to say, and I needed to think about what his words represented. All at once, he was telling me to stop feeling sorry for myself, stop crying on his shoulder, and to suck it up. It was the first time in a while I had been spoken to that way. There was no soft-stepping, no polish, and no apologies.

It's the best way to communicate with me. Just tell me straight up, "This is how it is and this is what I think." Now, I may disagree with what you have to say, but if you want to communicate with me, talk to me like that. That's what Tony did that night, and when I hung up the phone I remember thinking, "You know what? He may be right."

Before the conversation with Tony, I was inconsistent on why I was doing rehab. Sometimes it was for football and some-times it was to walk and sprint like anyone else my age. But there was no confusion about what I was doing and why I was doing it after speaking with Tony. It wasn't just him, but our conversation was the tipping point. In the same month I had spent time with two of the greatest athletes in history, visited physically and mentally tough soldiers, made strides in my rehab, and been told to go for it by my brother. Why did I have to stop playing football? According to whom? And why? There are other stroke survivors who return to their jobs, even though their jobs do not involve banging heads with 300-pound men once a week for three hours. I could see myself going back to work.

At one point in my rehab, Anne asked Jim Whalen how far I was behind my teammates in terms of a structured off-season program. He told her three weeks, and she was impressed that someone who had a stroke could be just three weeks behind players who hadn't. I asked her again about returning to football.

"All I can tell you is that there is no neurological reason why you can't play," she said. "But you need to talk to Dr. Palacios and Dr. Greer. You need to ask things like, 'When am I totally coming off the blood thinner?' and 'Has any athlete who has had the heart procedure ever performed at an elite level with the device in him?' You need to ask them if you can go back out there and take a whack on the head."

I needed to talk to them for medical clearance, but I needed to talk to my wife about home clearance. When she heard about my conversation with Tony, she was pissed at him. "I'm not very happy with Tony right now," she said. "He's your brother, but he is not the mother of your kids." She couldn't believe that he would suggest that I play football again. It wasn't quite time for The Conversation about my desire to return to football, but Heidi knew that I wasn't just mentioning an offhand remark from my brother. She understands our closeness and our similar viewpoints on a variety of topics. In effect, if Tony had it in his mind that I could play again, Heidi understood that I was at least in the same neighborhood—if not the same house. Worse for her, I really was convinced I could do it.

So that argument became the backdrop for a tug-of-war that lasted most of the spring. I wanted to play, she was fiercely against it, and neither of us was willing to budge from our position.

5

TENSIONS AT HOME

Heidi and I have been married for ten years, yet it seems that we've grown up together. We were immature when we got married—she was twenty-one and I was twenty-three—and in the first couple of years of our marriage we realized that it was going to be a lifetime of on-the-job training. Both of us have learned to appreciate the toast Heidi's parents give to each other on their anniversary. They smile, raise their glasses, and say, "How about we give it another year?" I don't know if the light-hearted approach is the reason they have worked, but they're doing something right: they've been together for forty years.

I can still remember the first time Heidi and I had to sit down and define what our marriage was going to be. Heidi was the volleyball coach at Walpole High School at the time, and she didn't get home from her game until seven-thirty in the evening. I had been home for a while, following football practice, and as soon as she walked through the door I said, "I'm starving. What are we eating?"

She shrugged and said, "Well, I guess we had better order some Chinese."

I told her that I needed her to cook for me, and she said that she needed me to respect that she had a team to coach. We argued—Heidi stayed up all night—and the next morning she called her mother to complain about me.

My mother-in-law, Vicki Bomberger, listened to what Heidi had to say and then gave a surprising response: "What did you think you were getting into when you married him? You want to show him you love him? Cook him dinner."

Cooking for me wasn't going to mean that we were no longer equals. It just meant that with her working and me working, there had to be a definition of roles. A couple of mornings after our argument, Heidi got up early and cooked eggs. I began to grow into my role, too. I had to consider that she had a job as well, and asking your wife what's for dinner after she has just spent a full day coaching a team isn't the most thoughtful thing to say. I do have traditional values, but there was a time when I was trying to merge the impossible. I was trying to be a family man and also the party guy I was in college. I had to be one or the other, and I knew which one I wanted to be. And that's a major reason I stopped drinking.

Of all the fights I've had with Heidi, none could match the length and intensity of the disagreement we had over my future as a football player. It wasn't one of those fleeting fights that come and go like a twenty-four-hour flu. It wasn't a fight that could be resolved with a conversation or two. It was something that went on for weeks. We would wake up and she would be mad that I was going to the stadium. And I'd be mad that she was mad. We would state our cases three times a day and never come to a resolution.

I kept trying to sell Heidi on why I suddenly wanted to play football in 2005. We are usually on the same page, so the prolonged stalemate frustrated me. I may have been trying to sell her on why I was ready to return, but I was an angry salesman. It was all so clear to me. I was reaching the point where Anne Jacobson felt that she couldn't do anything else with me. It was time for me to work with the Patriots' training staff: Jim Whalen, Joe Van Allen, and Dave Granito. My vision was getting better, so much that I could actually drive myself to the stadium. Before, I was picked up at home by a kid whom everyone called Joe C. He'd drive me to rehab and then bring me home when I was done.

Heidi was happy that I was getting better, but she was annoyed that rehab somehow turned into football training. She told me that it was starting to feel like a regular off-season, when I wake up and head to the stadium to run and lift weights. It was happening too quickly for her, and she felt like a bystander. If I was trying to persuade her to support my desire to play, Heidi was on a campaign to convince our family and friends why I should be stopped. She didn't have to work too hard, especially with the women, because they agreed with her.

This time her mother was not on my side; she thought I was crazy. "Guess what Tony told him," Heidi said to her mother. "Tony thinks he can play again. Easy for him to say when he's thousands of miles away in Vegas. He doesn't love him the same way that I do—this is the father of my children!" And when

Heidi told one of her best friends, Sharon Roberts, that Sharon's kids would have to start making good-luck cards for me again, Sharon didn't follow what Heidi was trying to say. Sharon's daughter, Abby, has always made me good-luck cards before games. I put one in my locker, and one of the TV reporters noticed it and did a story on Abby before one of our Super Bowls. So when Heidi explained that I was determined for the games—and cards—to return, Sharon was shocked.

"What is wrong with that boy?" she said.

It was a tense time for us, basically a month without hellos and good-byes. Heidi and I are very big on saying "Hey" or "How are you?" to each other often. If one of us walks in the door, the other is usually there with a kiss, a smile, or something. When I leave the house, I almost always hug her and tell her that I love her. If I get to the car and realize that I forgot something, I'll go back in the house, get what I'm looking for, and tell Heidi that I love her again.

There wasn't any of that for a month. We didn't have conversations. Instead, we exchanged half-sentences and minimalist statements. When I left the house, I would offer a terse, "All right, I'm going to the stadium." Her reply would be, "All right." And then I would leave. If Dante cried, the "conversation" would be, "Are you going to get the baby? Or do you want me to get him?" Usually, we love to spend time in Boston for a night of dinner and some type of show. There was none of that, either.

Even before our fight, I was having issues with going out. When I did, I could either see the pity that people had for me, or I could sense their awkwardness in not knowing what to say. And if anyone did have specific questions about me, I wasn't sure

I could give them the answer they wanted. Sometimes I didn't even know the answers myself.

As the fight went from hours to days and days to weeks, Heidi and I didn't want to socialize and pretend that everything was okay, because things weren't okay. "This is absurd," she said at least a dozen times. "Tony says you can come back, but I'm not your brother. I'm the mother of these three kids and you're the leader of this family. We almost lost you. How can you not see how dangerous this is?"

There were a few reasons I didn't see the danger. I felt physically stronger, even if I had to start over when it was time for me to lift weights again. For bench presses, I would start with lifting the 45-pound bar and then, in the beginning, work up to just 105 pounds. I also knew what I had been told privately by Anne and Dr. Greer. I asked them if I could play and they both said yes. But Heidi hadn't heard those conversations, so everything I said about playing football seemed outrageous to her. I asked her a few times to come and watch me work out so she could see for herself how close to normal I was. Heidi is naturally much more emotional than I am, and mentioning football wasn't helping. She would restate her position often: "You're the father of my kids, I don't want you to have another stroke, and I'm not having this return to football."

It was difficult and unusual for us to be at odds like that every day. For as long as we've known each other, it has never taken us long to understand what the other person needs. Heidi wanted to support me, but her instincts wouldn't let her do it. She kept saying that she needed to look Dr. Greer in the eyes and have him tell her what he had told me. Several months later she explained what her actual plan was: she thought it was a cinch that Dr. Greer would shoot down my idea, and a face-to-face visit with him would allow the doctor to talk some sense into me. So about ten weeks after we had been in the back of a speeding ambulance on our way to Massachusetts General Hospital, we were on our way there again. The first time, in February, we were a unified team determined to find the cause of a weakened left side, a massive headache, and a lack of vision. This time, we couldn't agree on what to do next, both of us essentially praying for Dr. Greer to endorse our side.

We both trusted Dr. Greer and felt that we could communicate with him. He wasn't much older than either of us, he was knowledgeable, and he had a sense of humor that could sneak up on you. He tells a great story about growing up in Florida, where his dad was a neurologist and his mom an advice columnist for a local newspaper. One day he was at home complaining about his girlfriend, telling his mother that the girl was acting "like a silly blonde." Apparently he didn't tell his mother that the information was off the record, so she put the story in the paper (with the names changed). His girlfriend saw it, wasn't fooled by the changed names, and immediately broke up with him.

Dr. Greer still laughs at himself when he tells that story more than twenty years later. He describes his own sense of humor as "rampant," but he had no idea that he was going to sit down with a couple whose smiles had either been forced or nonexistent for weeks. The doctor was about to be an arbitrator whose ruling, both Heidi and I hoped, would be final. I told Heidi that if Dr. Greer or any other doctor told us that I was being foolish, I wouldn't try to play. But I couldn't envision anything like that. I felt great.

Heidi walked into Dr. Greer's office with a list of concerns. She had questions for him, and she requested that all of his answers include the worst-case scenarios. She threw a lot at him. Leading up to the visit, she had prepared like a good attorney presenting a case. For a week, she had thought of and formulated very specific situations that she wanted Dr. Greer to discuss. She was on the edge of her seat for most of her questioning, truly measuring her words and carefully analyzing each response the doctor had. While she wasn't overly emotional, she was animated and did raise her voice a few times.

"Don't sugarcoat this, please," she said. "I want to know what we're up against. I want to know the truth."

Dr. Greer nodded. I sat calmly, even looking out of the office window at times. I knew this was obviously important for us as a couple, but I was in a different emotional place from Heidi's. I had doubts, but they lasted for split seconds and went away. Her doubts flashed constantly, and that led to her being overprotective and scared.

"Can the device in his heart move?" she asked. "If it does move, does he have a heart attack? Does he die on the spot? Does it bleed? What happens if he takes a hard blow to the head?"

As requested, Dr. Greer gave Heidi the answers in a straightforward, matter-of-fact way. He explained that the device in my heart shouldn't move. He said that while I'm at a greater risk than other players to have a stroke since I've had one already, I shouldn't be at risk because of the corrected PFO. That "shouldn't" was there a lot. I think we both got the point that there were no guarantees. Heidi had other questions, too.

"How is the travel going to be on him? Is he going to have to take blood thinners to travel? How is that going to affect the hits he's going to take during the game? Will he be able to take painkillers while he's taking blood thinners?"

There were some questions that Dr. Greer could not answer definitively. He even asked me what it takes for me to mentally and physically intercept a football. He wanted to know because, as he said, there is a lot of neurological activity involved, and he couldn't guarantee that I would be the same player when I returned. His overall point, in layman's terms, was that he believed I could play again. What really got Heidi's attention was the doctor's answer to her question about possibly delaying the decision to play by one year.

"Would that benefit his health if he waits a year to play?" she said.

"No," he replied. "The only difference is that he'll be a year older."

I looked at Heidi's face after he said that, and I could tell that she was stunned. The meeting didn't go anything like she planned. And as much as she respected the wisdom of Dr. Greer, hearing everything he had to say didn't make her feel better. She wasn't ready to register everything he said. She was happy to hear him say that I was a perfectly healthy person who was actually healthier than before due to the device in my heart. She nodded when he said that I could skydive, Jet Ski, and even play pro football. But a part of her wanted to take all the risks out of our lives. She told me to look at things from her perspective: she was a thirty-year-old woman with three young children, including a newborn, and one morning she'd had to rush to the hospital because her husband was having a stroke. Shortly after that, her husband had mentioned retirement before changing his mind and focusing on a return to pro football. She told me that February had scared her so much that sometimes she wanted me to live in a bubble. Coming back was too much, too soon for her.

Contrary to what we both believed, Dr. Greer's words did not end the conflict. We continued to hold on to our positions, and we took them from an old house to a new one. We moved from Red Oak Road in early May because we needed more space with our expanding family.

Something was going to have to change. I couldn't continue being so distant from Heidi. Although we had a disagreement, it didn't seem to be a situation where there was a gulf between us. We could certainly find a way to solve the problem, or at least get it to the point where we weren't being so short with each other.

One day in the new house, I went to the top of the stairs and sat next to Heidi. The tension had gone on too long, and now it was time for some relief. As opinionated as both of us were on the subject, we both felt awful about not being there for each other. I sat there in the near darkness and exhaled.

"I can't do this without you, babe," I said.

"And I can't hold you back from this," she said. "I feel like I'm not being supportive of your dreams and what you want to do."

It seemed like months since we had both exhaled. We were pleasant and at ease. It was the first constructive communication we'd had since April.

Before that conversation, returning to the Patriots was all or nothing for me. Either I was going to play in 2005 or I was going to retire. The words of Bill Belichick had passed me by when he mentioned them in early March, but they came back to me as I sat with my wife at the top of the stairs. Why couldn't I take a year off? Why not do that, be sure that everything was fine with my health, and bring peace back into the house? It wasn't the perfect solution, because Heidi and I both wanted something else, but it was a compromise that we could live with. It was a revelation to me. I was smiling and puzzled at the same time. How had Belichick thought of this quickly, while it took me months to get to this point? I had a lot of emotions all at once: joy, optimism, and a hint of befuddlement.

Once I decided to take the year off, it was a case of déjà vu: I planned to meet with Bill and Mr. Kraft, individually, to tell them the news. When I saw Bill, I was a completely different man from the one who had sat in his office and held back tears. I had been excited to go to the stadium that day, practically running out of the house to get there. I felt free; I felt that I now had a goal that was not going to cause any controversy in my house. My enthusiasm was noticeable when I told Bill that I could be like Mark Fields and take a year off. I told him that the PFO was closed, my rehab was going extremely well, and I was confident that I could resume my career. Bill smiled and commented that, if nothing else, he was glad to see me with so much energy and optimism.

My meeting with Mr. Kraft didn't go as smoothly, and it left me wondering if the owner of the team—and a friend to Heidi and me—was taking me seriously. I've always understood Mr. Kraft's perspective on the Patriots. He is the father figure, the caretaker of the organization. He is running the logo, not the name on the back of the jersey. If something were to happen to me, he would take a lot of heat. He looked me up and down when I told him of my plan to play football in a year.

"Tedy, I remember the conversation when you called me and told me you were retiring," he said. He repeated it a couple more times.

"I remember it too, Mr. Kraft," I said.

It was awkward. He told me he was going to make some phone calls because he wanted me to see some excellent doctors. To me, Dr. Greer was enough. I was comfortable with his care and advice, and besides, Mass General is one of the most respected hospitals in the country. I began to have some strange thoughts during and after my conversation with Mr. Kraft. The one that bothered me the most, and which I couldn't shake, was the feeling that he thought I was bluffing in order to get a paycheck. Did he think I was looking for an easy way to pick up next year's salary? I told Heidi what I thought, and she found it hard to believe. She feels close to Mr. Kraft and his wife, Myra, and that bond was strengthened when I was in the hospital. They were at Mass General almost immediately when I was admitted, and they came to visit twice during my three days there. Not only are they supportive of me, they go out of their way to ask about Heidi and our marriage.

So when Heidi heard that Mr. Kraft wanted me to visit Arthur Day, a doctor at Brigham and Women's Hospital in Boston, she didn't view it with skepticism the way I did. She was thrilled when she heard that we would be talking with another doctor. She knew Dr. Greer made a lot of sense in his explanations to her, but she wasn't emotionally ready to hear what he had to say. While she accepted my offer to take a year away from football, her preference was that I not play at all. For her, seeing another doctor was a way to gain more education and, possibly, hear someone say that returning to the game was ridiculous. That made sense to me, but I still didn't know what to make of the reaction I had gotten from Mr. Kraft. Was he telling me to see other doctors to make sure I was okay? Or was it something else? Those were the things going through my mind. I've seen guys milk injuries, and I didn't want anyone to think I was doing the same thing.

I was going to respect Mr. Kraft's wishes and see Dr. Day, but before I made that trip to Boston, I had some important business to finish up in Foxboro. I was going into my last session with Anne, the physical therapist from Spaulding. My final strength test with her was hamstring muscle strengthening. I was on my belly, lifting the left hamstring and then the right. I knew I had aced the test before I looked at Anne, and when I looked up at her she was smiling.

"Wow, you're equal and symmetrical," she said. "Everything is back to normal. Vision, strength, coordination, everything. Sensory problems? Gone. Your hip strength is back to normal."

We sat in my car for thirty minutes and talked about what I was going to do next. I told Anne that I couldn't thank her enough, not just for her physical help, but for her insistence on privacy and professionalism that was well beyond the norm. Her expertise is not athletic training, but she had listened well and researched the things she didn't know. I was impressed with that. She told me that she enjoyed working with me and hoped I

Me, ready for action in snow. I've always enjoyed playing in bad-weather games.

Classic pose after interception against Miami in 2003. This is one of my favorite moments in New England: I'm kneeling after my interception return for a touchdown against the Dolphins sealed the division title in 2003. Seconds later, the fans celebrated by flinging snow in the air each time they heard "Hey" on "Rock and Roll Part 2."

Embracing Tom Brady. Tom Brady and I have a relationship that goes beyond celebrating a victory, as we're doing here after the 2004 conference championship game in Pittsburgh. After the stroke, Tom and I became as close as brothers.

The celebrating linebackers. Me and my linebacking crew after winning the 2003 AFC championship game against the Indianapolis Colts. From left to right, standing: Tully Banta-Cain, Ted Johnson, Mike Vrabel, Willie McGinest, Matt Chatham, Larry Izzo. In front: Don Davis, Rosevelt Colvin, Me.

A new addition to our family. I'm with the family in Houston, celebrating our win in Super Bowl XXXVIII. From left to right: My brother, Tony, and his wife, Linda; Heidi; my mom; my sister, Natalia; and my stepdad, Ron.

Pointing out something to Bill Belichick. On the field and off, Bill Belichick has the ability to think logically and see the big picture.

Talking with Romeo Crennel. I have a lot of respect for Romeo Crennel, our former defensive coordinator. He put such an emphasis on team communication that he often told the defense, "If you're going to be wrong, at least be wrong together."

On the field with Robert Kraft. I've had many pleasant conversations with Patriots owner Robert Kraft, but one of the most awkward ones occurred when I told him that I was retiring.

Talking with Rodney. Rodney Harrison is the most physical teammate I've ever had. When he got hurt in 2005, I asked myself, "How am I supposed to play without him?"

Acknowledging the fans. The fans of New England have watched me grow as a player and as a man. I'm humbled and flattered each time I see someone wearing my jersey.

Carrying TJ and Rex. This is the perfect beginning to Super Bowl XXXIX: on the field with TJ (right) and Rex.

Gatorade on the Belichicks. Coach Belichick was able to avoid a Gatorade shower in our first two Super Bowl victories, but I was able to get him and his father, Steve, in the closing seconds of Super Bowl XXXIX.

On the field with TJ, Heidi, and Rex, postgame. TJ, Heidi, and Rex helped me cap my season by celebrating a 24–21 victory over the Philadelphia Eagles in Super Bowl XXXIX.

On the day I left Massachusetts General Hospital. I had problems with my vision and coordination. I couldn't see to my left, and I wouldn't have been able to stand if Heidi hadn't been there to hold my hand. Dr. Greer, in the white coat, is behind me, followed by Jim Whalen.

At the ring ceremony with Heidi, standing near three trophies. Like many couples affiliated with the Patriots, Heidi and I became very familiar with ring ceremonies at Mr. Kraft's home. My fingers tell the story here: this was our third championship.

The Big Four walking toward the Fenway mound. I had the privilege of celebrating the Red Sox' first World Series title in eighty-six years with (left to right) Bobby Orr, Bill Russell, and Richard Seymour. I'm wearing Boston manager Terry Francona's number 47 jersey.

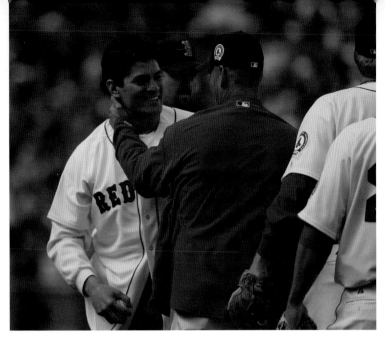

With Terry Francona. Terry Francona is teary-eyed as I wear his jersey on Opening Day 2005. Francona, the manager of the Boston Red Sox, sent encouraging notes and e-mails as I recovered from my stroke.

On the Meadowlands turf, being attended to by trainer Jim Whalen. With so much attention devoted to the stroke in 2005, it seemed that people forgot I could actually get hurt playing football. As soon as I went down here with a calf injury against the Jets, I said to myself, "This is at least two weeks."

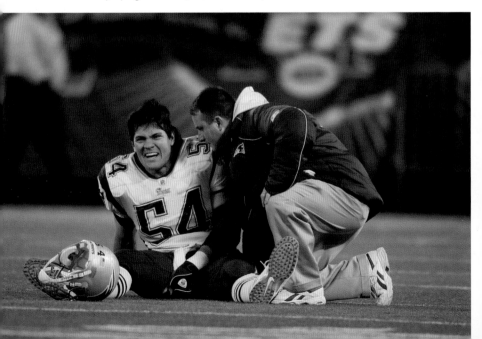

Defensive captains in San Diego. It's easy for me to be confident before a play-off game, like this one in San Diego, when I'm surrounded by captains such as (left to right) Mike Vrabel, Larry Izzo, and Richard Seymour.

Being congratulated by Mike Vrabel. Fellow linebacker Mike Vrabel is one of my best friends on the team. Mike is also the king of one-liners, so he's the only one who could get away with calling my heart "Swiss cheese" following my surgery.

would get back on the field. But, she said, she really didn't care what I did for a living.

"You're a good person," she said. "And to me that's more important than anything else."

I thanked her again, gave her a hug, and then she was gone. I had come a long way from the man who couldn't fully balance himself without holding on to Anne's shoulders. In a short time, I was able to legitimately think about lining up with my teammates again.

The meeting with Dr. Day was coming up, but I wasn't concerned about it. I knew that Heidi was at the point where she needed to hear the same things from different people, over and over. If she could hear it enough, she would be completely on board with it. I knew it would take a special person to say something to her and have it stick enough so that she would have no further worries. Dr. Day nearly became that person during a mesmerizing lecture in his office.

We drove there on a beautiful spring morning. His Boston office is on Francis Street, which is close to some elegant old buildings and majestic trees. I remember being excited by the entire scene. Heidi and I hadn't agreed on a lot in the previous weeks, but I knew she felt the same way I did when we finally met Dr. Day. It was evident that this friend of Mr. Kraft's was a big shot, a highly intelligent man with a folksy southern accent. He had our trust quickly, and although he had been tipped that Heidi had questions and concerns, he wouldn't let her talk for the first twenty or twenty-five minutes we were there. He spent that time educating us.

He took out a piece of paper and sketched my brain, the blood clots, and the blood flow. He then took us to his computer and showed us pictures of my brain and some MRIs.

"I'm trying to empower you two here," he said. "Education is a very powerful thing."

He then explained that the blood clot had entered my brain and then broken off into six different branches. Any one of those six could have taken my vision, my speech, or even my life. Heidi and I were taken aback. How was I even there? How was I even walking and talking? We both felt blessed and we knew that somebody was definitely watching over us. Dr. Day said that we were fortunate that the branches of the clots went to silent spots in my brain, spots that everyone has.

I wasn't sure where he was heading with his lecture, but I wasn't going to complain about it. He had a two-person audience, and we were hanging on each of his words. Then he got down to the empowerment. He pulled out another piece of paper and started writing down things that could have prevented me from playing football. He would write down a subject, such as the dissection of an artery, list three things that are symptomatic of a dissection, and then cross those three things out. He had used up an entire sheet of paper when it hit Heidi and me: none of the things he was talking about applied to me.

"Tedy, you had a stroke. *Had* a stroke, past tense," he emphasized in that southern drawl. "Just like you had your tonsils out when you were in college. That doesn't affect you now, just as your stroke doesn't affect you now. You addressed the issues that caused the stroke; therefore, you're as good as new."

112

It was the best thing that Heidi could have heard. I knew she was coming around when she looked at me and it was as if I could see the fear leaving her eyes. It was a look that seemed to say, "You're not going to die." I was learning so much, and not just from Dr. Day's illustrations. I was learning about the learning process itself. You have to be ready to hear certain information and you have to be in the right emotional state. The fact is that Dr. Greer said the same things to Heidi that Dr. Day did, but the conversations were weeks apart. Plus, Heidi is a visual person. I think Dr. Day's presentation won her over. He had more, too. Finally, he pulled out another sheet of paper. He wrote down two questions for us: 1. Can you live with it? 2. Will you be the same?

On the first question, he said that we were the ones who had to make the decision. Since we were the ones making it, he wanted to know if we could live with it. He is a smart man, so he had already spoken with Dr. Greer and he obviously knew we had. If we had spoken with our primary doctor and were still seeking other opinions, the reason was clear: we were uncertain. He said that whatever we did, we needed to be on the same page with it. He told us that we should think about what we wanted to do for six months before making a decision. "Your heart won't heal more in six months," he said. "You need about six months to make sure you're both emotionally okay with it."

As for being the same, Dr. Day said he couldn't answer that question. He was sure, as Anne had said, that my coordination was back to normal. But no one knew if I would still be able to master the intricacies of football. There is something that allows me to jump in front of a receiver and intercept a ball. There are some subtle motor skills that I don't spend a lot of time analyzing; a lot of it is instinct. No one knew if those skills would ever return.

When Heidi and I left Dr. Day's office, we felt like we had gone to see an inspirational speaker. He was able to educate, debunk, and advise all at once. The heavy atmosphere at home wasn't going to be necessary anymore. We were about to be a peaceful couple again, although neither of us knew how close we were to becoming a typical couple. That's because we left that idyllic scene in Boston and headed home to North Attleboro— without a map or GPS. We wound up on Boston's version of the autobahn, a winding road called the Jamaica Way, got lost, and argued over whose fault it was that we had to navigate through a maze of residential streets just to get home. At least that is the type of disagreement that pops up and then disappears in an hour or two. The longest fight of our lives, a fight that had lasted at least a month, was over.

That night I sat in my office at home, looking over some mail and doing some things online. Heidi walked into the office and sat across from me. She had a lot on her mind. She felt that I still had some animosity for her because she hadn't expressed her support for me the way Tony had. I don't know if it was animosity or if what I felt was even conscious, but as I've said, Tony knows how to challenge me with extremely direct language. Tony would have been proud of Heidi, because she used the same technique to make her point that night.

"I'm a strong woman, I can handle this, I'm not going to be a wreck when you're out there, and I'm supporting you," she said. "But this is not a movie. I think you want it to be like

Rocky and Adrian. This is my life. I can't be the one to slap you on the butt and send you out there. But I am strong and I'm going to be strong for you."

She sat there and talked for a while, and she covered a lot of areas. She said that I wouldn't have to worry about her reaction anymore and that we weren't going to discuss the pros and cons of waiting a year again.

"I think you feel that you've been carrying the burden by yourself, but you don't have to do that anymore," she said. "'Cause I'm here with you, and we can do this. I'm not holding back anything. I'm not against you."

It had turned into a day of incredible information and speeches. I thought Dr. Day would be an impossible act to follow, but Heidi had done it. She knew that a hundred doctors could clear me to play and it wouldn't make a difference if she wasn't convinced that playing again was the right thing to do. I needed the approval of doctors and therapists, but I needed her, too. It's something that has always been necessary in our marriage, and even more so since the stroke.

I once made a visit to Spaulding, and a woman who'd had a stroke approached me. She just said, "How did you do it?" And I wish I could have told her and other people that there's a pill you take. But it's not a pill or anything like that. She started crying and said, "'Cause I have three sons and I don't know what I'm going to do." I told her that those three sons are the ones she has to be strong for and the ones she has to lean on. She has to tell them when she's having a bad day and having a good day. Just communicate her feelings. Because being able to talk to Heidi and Tony, that's what really helped me.

Heidi talked to me that night in my office and I listened, but there were many times it was the other way around. She knew everything I was going through. I told her that there were times I even questioned the decision that caused our long fight. There were times when I was working out and I'd ask myself if Heidi was right. The workouts were challenging, actually harder than ever, and my heart was pounding in my chest. I needed to tell her that there was some doubt on my part.

She also could hear and see how much pressure I was putting on myself. I just felt that I was being watched at all times, and I couldn't fail under that scrutiny. I couldn't even describe what failure was to me, but I felt responsible for people I didn't know. In my mind, I was working hard for my extended family and for my sons. I was also trying not to let down other stroke survivors. It was too emotional and too undefined to carry and articulate by myself.

Dr. Day's simple question to us—"Can you live with it?"—turned out to be brilliant. It would become a refrain for us when we considered options. It would also be something we asked ourselves when, down the road, there would be much speculation and criticism of our family decision to play football. On the first night we thought about the doctor's question, our answer was yes. We could live with our decision and, for the first time in weeks, we could live easily together. I didn't know it, but it was apparently the perfect time to throw a party.

6

WANDERING

The official reason for my surprise party was the date: June 9, 2005, my thirty-second birthday. But this party, held at a nearly new golf course called the TPC Boston, truly could have been a celebration of everything in my life. I was surrounded by my friends, I was about to be healthy enough to stop taking blood thinners, the weekly debates with Heidi were behind us, and I was confident—or so I thought—that taking a year away from football was the right thing to do.

So a party at a world-class golf course was perfect and ironic. Heidi usually has a hard time sneaking a Christmas present in the house without me finding out about it, but she was able to pull off this surprise without me having a clue. I made it difficult, though. It was around the time of the Patriots' minicamp, and I didn't feel like I was a part of the team. Even though I was feeling much better physically, I still didn't feel that I had a football home. Heidi's plan was to have one of my teammates convince me to go golfing on a Saturday. Once that happened, I would wind up on the course with Tom Brady, Mike Vrabel, Christian Fauria, Ted Johnson, Josh Miller, Larry Izzo, and Dan Koppen. At least that was the plan. But when Mike asked me if I would golf with him on Saturday, I told him I was going to take TJ and Rex fishing. Christian tried next, and I told him the same thing. Christian tried so hard that he wound up calling Heidi and telling her, "I feel like I'm stalking him. I feel like such a nerd asking him to play so much."

I finally gave in. We got to the course and we played what some guys called the greatest round of golf ever. Playing a two-man scramble, we all teed off on the same box; it was eight guys on the box for every hole. Some guys had a thirty-pack of beer, and there I was drinking my O'Doul's. The conversations were great, and being around some of my teammates made me feel like I was one of them again. I hadn't felt that way in a long time, and on many days it seemed that no one could understand some of the emotions I had. I was happy playing golf with them, and I was even more elated when the round was over and the crew directed me to the clubhouse. I didn't even notice that they wanted me to walk in first and toward the bar.

There were a lot of people in the room, people I didn't know, and they were all staring at me. It was weird at first, and then it hit me just a few seconds later: I recognized several of my team-mates' wives, girlfriends, and even parents. Suddenly the entire room, even the people I didn't know, erupted with "Surprise!" I couldn't believe it. Everyone was there: Koppen's mom, who was in town visiting, Tom's girlfriend at the time, Bridget Moynahan, Rhonda Fauria, Jen Vrabel, Angie Miller, Maura Izzo, Jackie Johnson, and, of course, Heidi.

The club had set up a back room for us, and we all dug in to an excellent dinner. I was overwhelmed, because between the long disagreement with Heidi and my varying moods, I felt that we had been in a hole for months. I wanted and needed to be out and around that extended support system. I felt like I had to say something, so I stood and gave a short toast. I thanked everyone for being so supportive and for making Heidi and me feel so good.

The party was well timed, because it segued into another big event, one that would allow me to see everyone at once. Two days after the party, the team was scheduled to appear at Mr. Kraft's house for what had become a red-carpet happening. For many veterans on the team, it was going to be our third Super Bowl ring ceremony in four years. It seemed that as the trophies and rings accumulated, the ceremonies became more extravagant. Just as he had in the previous two events, Mr. Kraft had a red carpet leading to his front door. As you walked down it, he would be at the door to personally greet you. His beautiful green lawn was decorated with the Patriots' logo, the Boston University drum line was there to play, and a large tent was set up in the back for dinner and dancing. The rings made a dramatic entrance. They were held high above the crowd, like an ancient king being carried by his attendants. You could hear U2's "Beautiful Day" playing, and when the boxes containing the rings were opened, the music was drowned out by the various emotions from players and their wives and girlfriends. There were gasps, there were screams, and there were tears. It was the first ring of Corey Dillon's career, after eight frustrating years in Cincinnati, and it was obvious how precious it was to him. He cried, and so did Tom and Rodney.

Since the Patriots began the Super Bowl tradition of being introduced as a team, we continued it by opening our ring boxes as a team, too. But there was a twist to that in our family. I've always believed in the teamwork that I've had with Heidi. I look at how good and respectful and well-behaved our kids are, and I give her the credit for that. She is a great mother. There are times during the season when I can't be around and she is responsible for raising the boys. She is a part of the championships, too, so I don't open the ring boxes; I let her do it. There was such a sense of pride and accomplishment when Heidi opened the box and the gorgeous ring stared back at us. Out of the three rings that we have, I believe that the third one is the best. I held it with Heidi, and we were both ecstatic. It took both of us back to a time before the stroke, and it was good for us to do that—even for a moment—because the stroke had become so central in our lives.

Even though all the rings are dazzling, the stories lie in the journey to get them. To me, the rings are the whole season rolled into one. It's the smell of the grass. It's the kids. It's coming home late on away trips, going upstairs, and finding Heidi asleep. It's challenging my teammates to be better and having them do the same to me. Everytime I look at the rings, I re-live the joy of each of the season's victories. I feel the sting of each defeat. I feel the aches of every injury. I felt all of those things that night, and it was emotional because there was a possibility that this might be my last hurrah as a player. After all the players had gotten their rings, I got up and asked all the guys to huddle. We then did our breakdown, which is a call-and-response that ends with "Aww, yeah."

The temperature that night may have been stifling, and the mosquitoes may have hounded us—Heidi had a dozen bites— but we felt that we could let loose with our friends and relax. In addition to the BU band, a live band played old and new songs for us to dance to. It was almost like an adult version of prom night. We had gone to Mr. Kraft's house in a party bus with many of the other players, and afterward the plan for some people was to be driven into Boston to hang out some more. Heidi and I didn't do that, but we left the ceremony feeling that we had a real connection and some certainty about my future.

I obviously didn't know it then, but I was so certain because I was still a month away from participating in training camp. What I do know now is this: from afar, it's easy to say that you're going to be fine sitting out a year. It's easy to say that attending meetings as a de facto player-coach and working out will be enough to stay sharp and satisfied. I found out how challenging it was in late July and early August.

But before then, Heidi and I went to Tucson for a month. We saw some of our close friends from college and members of our family. Since we were no longer divided over playing football again, the people in the family who had initially taken Heidi's side were also supportive of a return. We gave our friends enough information to put them at ease, but we didn't share everything. After the news of my PFO procedure broke in

Tucson in March, I started to become selective about what I shared with people and with whom I was going to share it. I just didn't want things to leak out, and I asked the people closest to us to be as tight-lipped as they could.

The irony is that toward the end of our stay in Tucson, just before the start of training camp, a strange sequence unfolded. The Patriots already knew that I would be placed on the physically unable to perform list, also known as the PUP list. If a player is on the PUP list at the start of the regular season, he can stay there until Week 6. At that time, there is a twenty-one-day window in which the team and the player have to make a decision: either the player has to be activated, or he is going to be out for the remainder of the regular season. (If you're put on injured reserve—or IR—at any point in the season, whether it's Week 1 or 12, you can't return until the following year.) I was going to begin on the PUP and then eventually be moved to IR, which would mean I couldn't play at all in 2005. The only thing that had to be cleared up was the wording of a statement to the media. I talked with Stacey James, who's the Patriots' media relations director. He told me to spend the night thinking about what I wanted to say, and he would release it to the media the next day. When I talked to Stacey the next morning he told me that a Boston TV anchor named Chris Collins was reporting that there was a 90 percent chance I was going to play in 2005.

"Well, he's going to look stupid," I told Stacey. "It's kind of funny, but I do feel bad for him. This is already how it was going to go."

I don't know who gave Chris the information, but if it was one of my teammates I really can't blame them for the assumption. A few of them had seen me working out, and it may have been clear to them that I didn't look like a man who was running and lifting just to stay in shape. I had a purpose and a goal. It began as something that was a year away, but it started to become more urgent as soon as I left Arizona and arrived back in Foxboro.

I was in an unusual mental and emotional space, and I didn't know what to make of it. I was on the PUP, but I wasn't hurt. Usually hurt guys have a lot of rehab to do, but I was feeling good and could do a number of things. So thoughts started to creep into my mind like, "Who are you? Are you one of those guys, like former Patriot cornerback Tyrone Poole, where you can't wait for him anymore so you put him on IR? That's not who I am. But aren't I doing the same thing?" I talked to myself all the time, questioned myself, and wondered if my teammates, coaches, and ownership thought I was just trying to milk the team for a paycheck. Did they think I was stealing? Did they believe that I really was going to come back and play again? I overanalyzed every look I got and every comment that was made to me. I remember a player I respect, a young guy and a friend of mine, coming up to me and asking if I was serious about the comeback.

"Of course," I told him.

He looked surprised. "Man," he said, "I thought you were just trying to get paid."

It bothered me. Did anyone else think this was all a ruse to get paid for working out? Did they know that stealing a check is something I could never do or support? If a friend of mine was thinking like that or even wondering about it, what was going through other people's minds?

I tried to remind myself that I had had a stroke and that I shouldn't feel guilty about that, but I did wonder if I should have taken the year off. I looked at our inside linebackers and we had a variety of issues. Ted Johnson had retired at the beginning of training camp, Roman Phifer was gone, I had the stroke, and the new linebackers, Chad Brown and Monty Beisel, weren't familiar with the system. It was bad for the team and bad for me. I spent a lot of time drifting between guilt, confusion, and, at times, a lack of motivation.

I took several trips to TPC, trying to get some peace on the course. But I wasn't golfing well because I was thinking about what was going on with the team. I struck up a friendship with one of the members there, a great golfer named Chris Veglas. He had a zero handicap, was a good conversationalist, and he promised to fix my swing. I played golf with Chris and also bent his ear about how out of sorts I felt, knowing that I wouldn't be playing for at least a season. I quickly grew to respect him, not just as a golfer but as a great listener and family man (he has two young sons) as well.

There would be some normal moments when I sat in defensive meetings within earshot of my buddies Rodney Harrison and Mike Vrabel. Both of them had earned my respect soon after I met them. Rodney is an intimidating force. I've never played with anyone as physical as he is. He doesn't just tackle guys; he drives them into the ground. Then after they are down he gives them a forearm. He makes incredible hustle plays and has good instincts. In some of our most physical wins, a lot of us were just following Rodney's lead. As for Mike, he might be the most quick-witted and uncensored player on our team, a combination that usually leads to some jaw-dropping comments. He would actually joke about my stroke. If he noticed me not paying attention, he would bring it up. Or we'd be talking about playing golf together and he'd say, "Don't worry, Tedy, I'll give you a couple of *strokes*." He called my heart "Swiss cheese" because it had a hole in it and said I really played up my exit in front of the cameras when I left the hospital in February.

Part of the reason for the joking is that Mike and a lot of other players didn't see me when I was at my worst, so they couldn't conceptualize how bad I had it. By the time a lot of them saw me, I had reached the working-out stage. Another reason Mike talked to me in that way is that he knew our relationship was built that way. In some ways, we're kind of like brothers. Families are first with both of us; his two boys are about the same age as my oldest two, and our wives are good friends. We even bring family into our workouts: he'll be my spotter in the gym and motivate me by saying, "All right, Tedy. This set is for TJ and this set is for Rex." Sometimes we'll wear the same thing to work. When we go to restaurants, we have similar orders. There was a time we were at a Christmas party and got our plates from the buffet. When we put them down they were almost identical; we even put our horseradish on the same side of the plate.

I think Mike just wanted to make the job normal for me again. He wanted it to be more about football than the stroke. So while the joking was good at first, it got to be borderline spiteful and briefly put a strain on our relationship. He would talk about my heart and I would start bugging him about his new contract and how he let the money change him. We'd go back and forth during the meetings and breaks, and it would seem like normal to me. But we both went too far. I remember telling Heidi one night, "This dude is really starting to piss me off." He got to me and I got to him. We both knew it had gone on long enough, so as they say on the HBO show *Entourage*, we "hugged it out" one day at the stadium.

While Mike and Rodney supported me and got me involved by jokes and business as usual, Tom Brady and Don Davis were supportive with a different type of conversation. It's the kind of talking I didn't have with any other players. Don stands for a lot of things that I respect—he's a devout Christian—and he helps us all out with player programs. He has a lot of wisdom, and I felt that if I needed advice or someone to look at things deeply I could always go to him. Tom is really outstanding that way, too. We've had some very deep conversations about life, and there's no doubt that he knows more about me than anyone else on the team. He's someone that I've opened up to, and we've shared parts of our lives that we wouldn't normally share with everyone. There are times I'll read an incredibly thoughtful e-mail from him and I'll say to Heidi, "Who is this guy?" Tom is supportive on the level of a family member, and it's just remarkable to have that with someone who works with you.

I needed all the support I could get in July and August. Some days I would be in those defensive meetings and would actually feel like I was a part of things. I'd be in Chad's or Monty's ear giving them tips and coaching points, and helping them would make me feel good. But sometimes I would be in a meeting and lose my focus. I'd leave in midmeeting, just walk out of the room and head to the golf course. I just couldn't take it anymore. There were days I'd come into the meetings with my golf shirt on and my teammates would say, "Oh, we know where Tedy's going in a little bit." They knew that I understood everything that was being explained, yet I was in a position where I wouldn't be helping the team for a long time. Man, I was lost. I didn't feel like I was a part of anything.

Eric Mangini was our defensive coordinator then, and he's the type of coach who likes to ask a lot of questions to see if you're absorbing the material. He tried to keep me into things by asking me what I'd do with certain formations and personnel groups. I was there for him and gave him the correct answers. Sometimes. But then I drifted off, mentally first and then physically.

And that was everywhere, at home and at work. Heidi saw that I was going crazy—"twiddling your thumbs" is what she called it. I was a healthy football player on hold, so I tried to do more things around the house to make me less antsy. There were some kitchen chairs that made a lot of noise, and I decided I would use some of the downtime to fix the bottoms. I got a screwdriver, unhinged the bottoms, and then—*Pow*—I jammed my hand right into the screwdriver. I looked at my hand and saw that it was bleeding, the first time I had bled since the stroke. I was off blood thinners then, but I was taking baby aspirin. It's an anticoagulant—it keeps your blood flowing—and I looked at my hand and wondered if it would ever stop bleeding. It tripped me out a little bit. I called the trainers because it started swelling on the back side; Heidi called our friends the Robertses, and asked them to come over because she needed to take me to the hospital. "Do I need a tetanus shot?" I asked our trainers. "What about the swelling?"

Clearly, Heidi and I had overreacted. The trainers told me to clean it up and see them in the morning. I thought to myself, "If I reacted that way to a minor home accident, maybe I'm really not ready to be thinking about football." I went in the next day and got a lot of ribbing from the guys in the training room.

"What were you doing?"

"Trying to fix a chair!"

"Can't you get somebody to do that for you?"

I didn't hear the end of that one for a long time. In addition to the usual barbs from Mike, I was also getting them from Dan Klecko, one of our former defensive linemen. Mike and Dan are movie buffs who can recite random lines in the context of a normal conversation. You could make a comment about a remote control and both of them will come up with some actor or comic from the eighties who had something funny to say about remotes. Being around those jokesters guaranteed that I was going to be made fun of but, as the preseason games approached, I started to feel better. My body was healed and I didn't feel as lost as I had at the beginning of camp. I remember thinking that I was doing all right because these games didn't matter much. Yet I contradicted myself when we went to Green Bay and dominated the Packers in a preseason game. The Packers had beaten us when we went to the Super Bowl after my rookie year, 1996, and it's a loss that still gets to me. So whenever we can beat the Packers, even in a game that doesn't count, I think it's a good thing.

As the preseason came to a close, I still hadn't talked extensively with anyone in the media. There was speculation about what I was going to do and various opinions on what I should do, but no one knew for sure. On September 1, exactly a week before we were scheduled to play the Oakland Raiders in the season opener, I sat down for a long interview with Jackie MacMullan, a *Boston Globe* columnist for whom I have a lot of respect. I've gone in depth with Jackie on a variety of subjects, including my reasons for giving up drinking. She came to our house and talked with Heidi and me about the night when our lives changed unexpectedly. The next day she had a lengthy front-page article that was headlined "Bruschi Plans to Play Next Year." If I hadn't already learned how quickly things could change in less than a week, Jackie's article was a classic example. Early in her story, she wrote that I "emphatically denied" that I would return to the Patriots in 2005. I was quoted as saying the following: "I'm telling you right now that's not going to happen. I need to do what's best for my family and myself. There's a difference between living life normally and being fine and getting ready for a professional football season. I need the year to get myself ready. I considered playing this year. We talked about it a lot. But this is something you don't rush. It's not a sprained ankle. . . . [The year off] will help medically, but it will also help me deal with it mentally. I think I've healed faster physically than I have emotionally."

What I told Jackie was true, and she quoted me accurately. But the story would have been different if I had talked with her five days later. I went for my six-month checkup with Dr. Greer on September 6, two days before the Raiders game. My echocardiogram was flawless, and Dr. Greer repeated his belief that the only physical difference between playing in 2005 and playing in 2006 was age; I would be a year older. Dr. Day from

Brigham and Women's had told us about waiting six months so we could be certain about the decision we were making, and it hadn't been six months. But the more Heidi heard doctors give me glowing reports about my health, the better she felt. That's all she had wanted and needed: she needed to hear doctors tell her, repeatedly, that I was going to be fine. Both of us had increased our stroke education level at least tenfold since the spring. So, for example, we knew how ignorant it was to suggest that playing football again would lead to another stroke. We knew what had caused the stroke, and we knew everything that had been done to repair and rehabilitate me.

The six-month echo in September was incredible. All we heard was, "You're looking great, Tedy. Everything is neurologically fine." It was early when we left Dr. Greer's office, no later than seven or eight, so I asked Heidi if she wanted to get breakfast. She said she did, so we drove from Boston to one of our favorite places in North Attleboro, A&J's. There wasn't a lot said during the drive, but I know both of us sensed that something significant had just taken place. There is no way I could have had a more positive and upbeat health report than the one Dr. Greer had just given. When we got to A&J's, I was feeling so great about my health that I decided to splurge and order something with a little grease and fat: I had blueberry pancakes with butter on top, a side of corned beef hash, a glass of orange juice, and some coffee. Heidi had chocolate chip pancakes. We sat in a booth and considered everything that we had been through.

"What am I waiting for, Heidi?" I asked her. "Physically, there is nothing wrong with me. Mentally, all right, I might be a little messed up in the head. But what am I waiting for?"

We weren't arguing. Heidi knew everything I did about my health. She knows me better than anyone, so she could see how much things were bothering me, from not being able to participate to the "I thought you were just trying to get paid" comment from a teammate.

"I know," Heidi said. "I know that you're fine."

We looked at each other across the table. We were about to come to a decision in our neighborhood diner.

"Let's just go for it this year," I said.

Heidi agreed that waiting one year didn't make a lot of sense. It was time to resume my career in 2005. I didn't have to wander about on golf courses anymore, asking myself what I was doing. I didn't have to fight myself anymore, asking what the purpose was of taking notes in 2005 for something that I couldn't do until 2006. No more; it was time to play.

Bill Belichick had Oakland on his mind, but I went to see him in his office to tell him the news. I told him that I wanted to stay on the PUP list until I was eligible to practice and play with the Patriots.

"Bill, I want to take advantage of that practice time," I said.

"Let me get this straight," Bill said. "There's still no way of you playing this year at all?"

I just looked at him. There was a pause, and he looked at me with raised eyebrows.

"Bill, I want to practice because I'm going to play this year," I said.

It's the first time I've ever seen Bill with a look on his face that let you know you said something he didn't expect. We're talking about the man who is always thinking ahead, two or three steps ahead of you. He's the one who mentioned the year off in the beginning when I wasn't thinking that way. Now it didn't appear that he had anticipated what I was going to say to him. He went over the gist of what I said, just to be sure he heard me say it.

"I want to make sure we're on the same page here," he said. "Are you telling me that going out there and picking up another linebacker this year would be the wrong move?"

"Yeah," I said. "That would be the wrong move."

Bill had seen me in all phases of my comeback. He talked to me when I thought I had to retire, he saw me when I told him I was going to take the season off, and he had to sense the joy I was feeling when I told him I was returning in 2005. I left his office and headed up a flight of stairs so I could see Mr. Kraft. I've never had a problem communicating with the owner of the team, and now we were talking more than ever. Each time I had something to report, I'd make a point to personally tell Bill and Mr. Kraft so they could stay in the loop. Mr. Kraft has always realized how important Heidi is to me and how we figure out issues together. So before he told me what I had to do, he asked a good question.

"Is Heidi on board with this?" he said. "I'd like to know what she thinks."

I told Mr. Kraft that Heidi was comfortable with me playing again. She had begun her path to comfort after Mr. Kraft told us to see Dr. Day. Both of us had been impressed with his knowledge, confidence, and charisma. He had sat us down and spoken to us in a way that began to make a believer out of Heidi. As a couple, we had come such a long way in a short time. As a stroke survivor, I had come a long way as well, and I felt that I had to be a strong representative for everyone who was watching me. Retiring or even waiting was no longer an option.

"You have one more person to see," Mr. Kraft said. "And you can take my plane to see him."

That person was Matthew Fink, a doctor at the prestigious NewYork-Presbyterian Hospital/Weill Cornell Medical Center. I knew where Mr. Kraft was coming from. As the owner of the team, he had to be as cautious as I was. As he said, he wanted me to "measure nine times and cut once." He had already sent us to consult with some tremendous doctors, at some of the country's finest institutions. Going to see one more doctor in New York was not going to be a problem, because I knew that this visit would be a formality. None of the visits was a waste of time, because they gave me and Heidi a chance to educate ourselves more, but we had gotten to the point where we knew what the doctors were going to say. There was no reason to be afraid.

We made a quick trip to New York to meet with Dr. Fink. It was stress-free for us, and we spent most of the time on Mr. Kraft's plane laughing and joking. We knew the trip was more for the owner than for us, so we were as relaxed as we had been in months. We got to Dr. Fink's office early, so we had an hour or so to burn before my examination. The wait didn't bother us, because we viewed the trip as a one-day retreat where we could just talk and have some time alone. There was a downpour in New York that day, so we borrowed an umbrella and went to a pub where the food was just awful; we even laughed about that. Dr. Fink finally examined me, and said he would talk with me more when I got back to New England.

I remember one phone conversation I had with Dr. Fink at the stadium. He had told me earlier that he was going to talk with some of his colleagues and get back to me. It's another reason I felt confident; it wasn't as if I had been basing my decision on one doctor's opinion. I was getting opinions from doctors I had met and others I hadn't. Not one of them had anything negative to say. So when Dr. Fink called in the locker room, I went into a quiet space so I could hear him.

You never plan for life to be so poetic, but it just so happened that the place I went to listen better was the same place where I couldn't focus a month to six weeks earlier: the meeting room. I closed the door behind me and sat in one of the theater-style seats. It was such a contrast of sounds, because I had just left a buzzing locker room and now I was sitting alone in perfect silence. I heard Dr. Fink clearly.

"You can pursue your life any way you want, professionally and personally," he said. I smiled and knew from that moment on that there would be no more doubts. I was going to play, try to meet the three consecutive Super Bowl challenges that Tom Brady had put to us at the Pro Bowl, and try my best to use my status as a pro football player to raise stroke awareness in the United States.

I was at ease with my decision on the Thursday night the Patriots played the Raiders. I hadn't announced anything publicly, so most people still thought I was going to be on the sidelines until 2006. Before the opener began, I was approached by Raiders running back Lamont Jordan. He told me that players around the league were praying for me, and he hoped to see me back on the field soon. It was a kind and generous gesture, and

I was moved by it. My old linebackers coach Rob Ryan, the Raiders' defensive coordinator, also had some nice things to say before the game. I'm not sure if they all realized it, but the people I heard from—in person, by phone, or by letters and e-mail—were a source of strength. They were not members of my family, and I obviously didn't go to them when I was having bad days, but their sincerity and kindness touched me.

As I watched the beginning of our game against the Raiders, I imagined that I was on the field again. The Raiders took the opening drive down the field, and as they approached the red zone, I felt like we were back in the 2004 Thursday-night opener against the Indianapolis Colts. On that night, the Colts drove near the goal line and I shouted to my guys, "All right, they're not going to score. Let's step up and make a play." I wasn't necessarily talking about myself that night, but when Peyton Manning dropped back to pass, I got a great read on where he was going and intercepted the ball at our 1-yard line and returned it 5 yards to our 6. But this was going to be a new experience for me. All I could do was mouth the words, "Let's make a play . . ." I couldn't step on the field, and so it was frustrating to watch Oakland score that first touchdown. I thought, "Maybe there is something I could have done to help." I stood and watched that game, a 30–20 Patriots win.

When Heidi watched the team run onto the field with me standing on the sideline, her eyes welled with tears. It was tough, but I understood that I would have to do the same thing for five more games until I could get myself into football shape and, finally, ready to play.

IT'S ALL ON US

As the team began preparing for Week 2, I was approached by Bill Belichick's assistant, Berj Najarian, and asked a question that he's rarely had to ask and I've rarely had to answer: "Do you want to go to the next game?"

The next game was in Charlotte against the Carolina Panthers. I had talked with Bill about my stroke, my heart procedure, my retirement, my desire to play again, and the six-week strength program I was going to use to get back on the field. But we had never talked about my personal "game plan"; was I going to travel with the team or not? It was September, and I had been on planes several times since the stroke, so I no longer had a fear of flying and developing another blood clot. I decided to travel and support my teammates against the Panthers, a team we beat in February 2004 to earn our second Super Bowl trophy. But a few days before the second game of the season, it was more important for me to be a supportive big brother than a supportive teammate.

My sister, Natalia, was engaged to a man she had been seeing for several years. He had been battling cancer in the beginning of their relationship. The cancer went into remission, and then it came back shortly after they got engaged. Early in training camp, I had gone to Los Angeles to see them both, when the physical toll on Natalia's fiancé began to be pronounced and noticeable. Unfortunately, his condition reached a point where it was just a matter of time for him. He died a couple of days before the Carolina game.

I felt for his family and was sad for Natalia. I didn't have a lot of energy and enthusiasm to give the team after that, so I didn't think it was a good idea to make the trip. The only teammate I talked to about the situation was Tom Brady. Tom's girlfriend at the time was the actress Bridget Moynahan, who has been in movies such as *I, Robot* and *Coyote Ugly*. Because Natalia does hair and makeup for many celebrities, she has developed a friendship with some of them, and Bridget is one of those friends. Both Tom and Bridget knew what was going on with Natalia's fiancé, and Tom talked to me about it at length. As usual, he was encouraging and supportive at a time when there really isn't a right thing to say. I know I was in an extremely reflective mood that week, but I can't say for sure that it was my mood that led to another decision: I wasn't going to travel to any of our games until it was time for me to play. It was the right decision for me. Most of the time, players don't travel if the team doesn't plan for them to play. There are some exceptions where a guy is questionable and playing is a game-time decision.

I wasn't in that category; it was strictly a countdown to Week 6 for me.

I had a lot of work to do to get ready, and I was trying to bring the same intensity to the workouts as Mike Woicik, who is the Patriots' strength coach. Mike has been the strength coach for the last two NFL dynasties, the Cowboys in the 1990s and the Patriots in the twenty-first century. He is so organized and meticulous that when Bill was interviewing candidates for the then vacant job in 2000, Mike blew him away with a detailed presentation of how he was going to install a program that would maximize the skills of each player on the team. You can find anything you're looking for in Mike's strength manual: he tells you what food to eat, he tells you what time to eat, he tells you what exercises are best for quarterbacks, kickers, cornerbacks, and linebackers, and because he knows that some athletes might be tempted to go out at night rather than study or sleep, he even tells you how much energy is expended dancing at nightclubs.

Mike's workout is challenging if you do it at a regular pace, and even harder when you try to jam everything you need into a six-week window. I watched the calendar constantly. I knew I was eligible to come back on October 30, a game against the Bills that had already been scheduled for Sunday night on ESPN. For me to be ready, I was going to have to roll the off-season program and training camp into one. I mentioned earlier that the conditioning test for linebackers consists of two sets of ten 50-yard dashes run at seven seconds each with thirty seconds of rest in between. Mike didn't have me pass the test just once over the six weeks; he wanted to be sure I could pass it four or five times. There were lots of position-specific exercises, also known as metabolics. For example, you have a card with ten exercises on it. One of them might say, "Simulate a 10-yard hook drop to the right," and you do that as a football is thrown at you. Or you might be told to run a 40-yard wheel route, which is when the running back runs sort of a curving pattern out of the backfield to the flat and up the sideline. You might do that for four or five sets of ten.

The conditioning run wasn't a problem for me on my way back, and it wasn't a problem before the stroke. But the metabolics were tough because I had lost so much upper- and lower-body strength. I had to start from the bottom and work my way up when it was time to lift weights again. The good news is that I went into each session with my highest level of concentration. I knew I had to get into great shape because this was going to be the first time in my life that I just jumped into a season without playing any exhibition games and going through a traditional training program.

Sometimes my workouts would be held in the practice bubble and would overlap with the team's workouts. There were times when I could feel some of my teammates looking at me, wondering what the hell I was doing. It was weird. I remember walking through the locker room once and looking at Rosevelt Colvin, one of our linebackers. Rosey has a way of making a face, a face that lets you know that he knows what's going on. I could just hear him saying, "What are you doing, Bruschi? I know what you're up to." I still hadn't told anyone of my plans, but there was something unspoken with Rosey and I got the feeling that he was in on the secret.

But the more I thought about this "secret," the more I felt

compelled to tell some of my teammates what was going on. While I didn't want any information to leak out to the media and create a distraction for the team, I didn't want something worse to happen. And to me, having my teammates misunderstand my motives was worse than any media exclusive. I needed them to know that I wasn't trying to get over, that I wasn't trying to milk management, and that this wasn't some mock effort so I could set myself up for retirement. I think a few of them started to figure it out anyway, but I didn't want there to be any confusion. Honestly, I was surprised that members of the New England media didn't figure out what I was trying to do. They would see me in the locker room just as I ended my workouts or began them. Once, Ron Borges of the *Boston Globe* even said to me, "Hey, you look like you're slimming down." I answered with, "I am. It's from all this running I've been doing lately." I wonder if he thought I was talking about running a lot for the *next* season. I was serious and passionate about coming back, and a few people—on my team, not in the media—needed to know that.

After we lost 27–17 to Carolina, I did tell Tom and Don Davis. Don's reaction was funny. "Maaaaan," he said. "I knew it! There's one day I saw you in the bubble and I said to myself, 'It looks like Tedy B. is trying to get himself ready to play this year.'" He couldn't stop smiling, and when he congratulated me I could feel how sincere he was. When I told Tom, he said it gave him chills, and he talked about how important and significant the comeback was. Mike Vrabel and Dan Koppen also knew about the return. Vrabel gave me a bear hug when he heard the news. I told Koppen on a golf course and he immediately envisioned the atmosphere at Gillette against the Bills. "Dude," he said, "that place is going to be rockin'. It's going to be awe-some." I was a team captain and team contributor, but I knew that coming back meant a lot more to stroke survivors than it did to our team.

Still, I was crushed in the third game of the season when our plan to win three consecutive Super Bowls took a major blow in Pittsburgh. At the end of a play, a Steelers receiver inadvertently rolled into Rodney Harrison, and Rodney fell awkwardly to the field. I watched it on TV and knew that it was a serious knee injury. Rodney tore three ligaments in his knee and was going to miss the entire season. This is how special Rodney is as a player: I actually asked myself out loud, "How am I going to play defense without him?" I had gotten used to his presence in 2003 and 2004, and I respected the way he took control of all the younger defensive backs and kept them in line. He pulls those guys aside and tells them what they should be doing to get the proper hydration and sleep. He tells them how to watch film and how to practice. He is in their ears a lot. Rodney is so talented and dependable that, as a linebacker, you never have to worry about anything going on behind you.

I knew on-field communication could be a problem with yet another veteran and captain out of the lineup. We trusted each other so much and had such an understanding of what everyone was supposed to do that we never had to repeat ourselves on the field. As the "Mike," or middle, linebacker, I'm responsible for making calls. But there are times when I don't really have to give the rush call because guys already know what to do. It's an advantage for our team, because it allows me to take my communication to the next level.

I'll give you an example. Let's say I'm giving instructions to "Ray" and "Leo," which is code for the right outside linebacker (Ray) and left outside backer (Leo). If I say, "Leo, Leo," that means the left backer is rushing. If I say, "Ray, Ray," the man on the right knows it's him. Now, here's the best part about shouting out the calls: my teammates already know what they're supposed to do before I say anything, but sometimes they like to hear it. It's their way of getting a little recognition and hearing that everything is all right.

When I wasn't practicing, some players would come up to me and say, "Bru, it's just not the same without you making the calls." I understood what they meant. Something unsettling happens when there is a cog missing in a successful defense. Not only are you taking away a playmaker, you're also not getting to the next adjustment level—which is really the next level of playing ball. Every Mike has similar thoughts: You think about the formation and what tendencies the team has out of that particular formation, and you look at the stance of the linemen and ask yourself, "Okay, what are they giving away?" If I have to worry about other players being in the right position, it takes me away from some extras that I might be able to focus on so I can get tipped off to what's coming next. When everyone is comfortable, I can look at my opponents' eyes. I can listen to the quarterback's cadence. I can listen to the audible and tell myself, "He said 'Black 45' on the audible, and that's a run to the right side. So if that happens again, I know what to do."

Another key is the ability to be accountable for your own mistakes and stay calm when things break down. Seven or eight years ago, we used to have arguments in our huddle. There would be an 8-yard run and guys would start screaming, "That's too much!" Well, that doesn't happen anymore. Because it's such a veteran group, we're constantly focusing on the bottom line—did they score or not?—and reminding each other of the game situation. You have to know how to talk to people with respect, even when you're a captain. To me, leadership isn't punking people in front of a crowd and grabbing a face mask. As a leader, you have to realize that the people you're leading are equals.

Take Richard Seymour, for example. He's the best defensive lineman in football, so offensive linemen often attack him with dirty moves to see if they can upset him. Sometimes, early in his career, they got him to lose his composure and he got a 15-yard penalty for shoving his hand in someone's face. I never say anything like "Settle down" to him when he's like that. It's foolish communication at that point, because it's not what he wants to hear. I'd get in his face and ask him if he's all right. He'd say yes, and that would be it. It's my way of talking and my teammates get it. When I ask him if he's all right, he knows what I'm really saying is, "Are we going to have a problem like this again? Are you focused on the next play?"

That's how smooth communication is supposed to go, but things weren't unfolding that way early in the 2005 season. At times I felt that I had abandoned my teammates as they struggled on defense. Our middle linebackers, Chad Brown and Monty Beisel, weren't picking up our system quickly enough to communicate in it, so Mike Vrabel, who can play outside as well as inside, was used exclusively inside to stabilize the middle of the field. It was also clear that our secondary wasn't the same without Rodney. Overall, we weren't preventing big plays and forcing

turnovers like we were used to. By the time I was eligible to practice and be activated, our record stood at a disappointing 3–3.

Our third loss of the season came on a Sunday afternoon in
October that I'll never forget. It was the third Sunday of the
month, and Heidi and I sat on our family room couch and
watched the Patriots and Denver Broncos on TV. There was confusing communication happening on the field and off. On the
field, the Broncos showed why they were a team that had won
four of their first five games as they built a 25-point lead. I was
thousands of miles away and I could see that the defense wasn't
communicating at a high level. In the second quarter alone,
Broncos quarterback Jake Plummer found Rod Smith for a
72-yard pass play and Ashley Lelie for a 55-yarder. In that same
quarter, a young running back named Tatum Bell sliced our
defense for a 68-yard run.

It was tough for me to watch, and I shifted anxiously on the
couch. I was tired of being a fan, sitting by helplessly as my teammates needed familiar bodies and voices to plug playmaking and
communication holes. We were down 28–3 in the third quarter,
but we made a comeback and actually cut the lead to eight,
28–20, with eight minutes left in the game. But we were done
for the day and, scheduling-wise, for another week. We had a
break after our sixth game, which was going to give some
players a lot of time to rest and heal up; it was going to give me
an extra week to practice and continue to regain strength. Our
early schedule had been the toughest the league could throw at
us: four road games at the Panthers, the Steelers, the Falcons, and
the Broncos. The Raiders at home was not a tough game, but the
Chargers came to Gillette and jumped us, 41–17.

As bad as the Broncos game was, it wasn't the only thing from Denver that bothered me that day. During the game, the Patriots released statements about my return to the NFL. I understood that something needed to be said, especially since I had told Jackie MacMullan of the *Boston Globe* that I planned to practice in the next week. The team didn't want me to make that announcement until they could do it officially, but it was hard for me to hold back. I had been holding so much in for so long, it was tough to contain my excitement when Jackie called and asked about the rumors of my return. I confirmed that I was going to practice, and she wrote the story.

So it didn't surprise me that the Patriots released two statements during the game. They had to say something because the story was already out there in print. What surprised me was the contrast in the statements. One was emphatic, upbeat, and unapologetic. The other one was cold and seemed to suggest that if anything went wrong, it was all on me.

Here is the more supportive statement, from Dr. Greer:

> I have had the opportunity to care for Tedy Bruschi since the day of his stroke eight months ago and have closely monitored his rehabilitation and remarkably rapid rate of recovery. Physically, Tedy is completely back to normal, and is exceptionally healthy. I have no doubt that he will be able to perform physically at a very high level. Tedy's safety, on and off the field, has always been our number one priority. At this time I have advised him that, in my opinion, there are no medical reasons for him to delay his return to football. Tedy has asked me not to discuss these

matters with the media further, and I will obviously honor that request.

I was impressed with Dr. Greer's statement on the surface, and even more amazed when I found out what went into it. It turns out that he thought he would have until Tuesday to write it, but he was approached on the Sunday of the Broncos game and told that it needed to be done then. So he was writing on a deadline, and he had to give everything he wrote to Mass General's legal and public relations departments so they could see where he was going with the statement. He would write a few sentences and then page the legal department, just to make sure he wasn't saying something that could get him or the hospital in trouble. The hospital was cautious because if something happened to me, everyone was going to make comparisons. Dr. Greer would be Gilbert Mudge, the cardiologist whose favorable medical opinion of Reggie Lewis flew in the face of a "Dream Team" of doctors that had been assembled by the Boston Celtics. And I would be Lewis, Dr. Mudge's celebrity patient who collapsed and died on the Celtics' practice court in the summer of 1993. Dr. Greer put his career on the line for me in that statement. And although each of his words was checked and rechecked by the hospital's lawyers, it didn't read like a legal document. I really appreciated how enthusiastic and direct it was.

In other words, it had all of the elements that the other statement, from the Patriots, did not. I'm sure the Patriots had their lawyers studying their document, just as Mass General did with Dr. Greer's words. But this time I could sense the legalese hovering over the words:

The New England Patriots have been advised that Tedy Bruschi has received unanimous medical clearance from outside specialists in the field of stroke neurology. He has also passed multiple physical examinations by team doctors and has been cleared to resume practicing as early as this week. The Patriots organization is satisfied that Tedy Bruschi has received the best medical attention possible and has been assured that he is medically cleared to resume his playing career. Tedy Bruschi has worked very hard throughout his rehabilitation to return to full health and has been assured by all who have examined him that he has. With the necessary unanimous medical clearances to return, Tedy Bruschi and his family will make the final decision as to whether he returns to the field and begins practicing once again with the team. The Kraft family and the entire Patriots organization want only what is best for Tedy Bruschi and his family and will continue to support his decision.

I understand business. I understand that the words had to be careful because the organization had to protect itself just in case something happened. But I'm human, and I knew what was being said to me behind closed doors and what that statement was saying. They didn't match up. The statement confused me. I reported back to the Patriots after I saw every doctor, and they knew what doctors I was seeing. Yet Dr. Greer's statement was as clear as day while the Patriots' statement seemed to say, "Hey, it's on him. It's his decision." As I've said, the Krafts are friends of ours, and they remained good friends—in private. Publicly, the organization came out with a cold-hearted statement, one that you would expect from a cautious billion-dollar business. I was taken aback as I heard and saw it. When I heard the last sentence of the statement being read on TV, I turned to Heidi.

"You know what, babe? It really is you and me. It's all on us," I said. "We have to be strong because a lot of people aren't going to understand where we're coming from."

We then had a discussion about being in the position to break through some walls, open some eyes, and educate people about stroke. "I want to be someone who makes people see what's possible after having a stroke like mine," I said.

When I spoke with Heidi about outsiders and their understanding of my return to the field, I was just speaking from the heart. I had no idea that the first wave of criticism would be so loud and, at times, so personal. I was too close to the story because I *was* the story, but I had thought things would play out differently. To me, coming back was about overcoming obstacles and challenges in life. It was about releasing that stigma of *stroke* and how people think you are totally different after you've had one. It is the number one disabler in the United States, but it doesn't mean you can't get your life back. People hear the word stroke and fear gets into their bodies because stroke is something that takes you away—like that. There's no warning. When I first heard the word, I had the same feeling. I couldn't even say it for a while because it was so shocking that it actually happened to me. My sons are too young to understand what I've done, but this is something I'm going to share with them when they are older and have tough moments in their lives. It's not something I'll throw in their faces whenever they stumble, but I do want to give them a living, breathing example of what can happen when you confront a tough situation and get through it.

That's what coming back was to me, and I thought it was clear when I gave my own press conference and emphasized the words *unanimous clearance*. I thought that was the phrase that would end all arguments and debates. I didn't think the majority of people understood what I was doing and why I was doing it. I talked to Stacey James, who is excellent at handling media issues as well as keeping an accurate media pulse. Stacey watched the TV shows, listened to the radio, and read the articles. He knew the same thing I did: the majority of people thought I was nuts. "It's sort of going differently than I thought it would go," Stacey said of the coverage. Instead of people being supportive, a lot of them were critical. There was no official poll, but it felt like 70 percent of the people were against what I was doing. It was tough to deal with because I didn't want to talk to a lot of my teammates; I felt like they didn't understand, either.

The criticism was national and local. On ESPN, three ex-NFL players all gave three versions of the same opinion: I shouldn't be playing. Michael Irvin said the Patriots should have taken the decision out of my hands and put me on injured reserve, ending my 2005 season. Steve Young said that a player, no matter how well-intentioned, cannot make the right decision. He said, "I pray for the doctors and the ownership to take [the decision-making] away from him and make the best decision." Dr. Greer was hot over Young's comment because he didn't like the inference that my doctors were allowing me to do a bad thing. As far as Dr. Greer was concerned, he didn't clear me to play; I cleared myself to play because, across the board, all the doctors had declared me to be neurologically normal. Finally, Tom Jackson said something that most people had in the back of their minds. He said it and they thought it simply because they didn't know better. Jackson wondered what would happen in a worst-case scenario. He wondered what would happen if "we're watching some Sunday afternoon and something happens to Tedy Bruschi on the field. You tell me how the league and the Patriots are going to feel the moment that happens."

I swear, I heard some of that stuff and I was thinking, "All of these critics are a bunch of cowards because they're basically saying what they would do in a situation like this." I don't know if they've had adversity in their lives, but when times got tough, they would have put their tails between their legs and tried to run away from the challenge that they had in front of them.

But the critics kept coming, from all directions. For the first time in my career, I think I appeared in the *Boston Globe*'s serious section, also known as the op-ed pages. Columnist Joan Vennochi used me to make a point about famous athletes and entertainers who have a hard time walking away because fame is seductive and we live in a hero-worshipping culture. Ron Borges wrote an article titled, "If This Backfires, Don't Blame Team." In the story, Borges wrote, "Bruschi has carefully orchestrated a media assault on Kraft and the Patriots, skillfully backing them into a corner by leaking just enough about his improving physical condition and desire to return to the field to leave Kraft with few options but to go along." Some athletes will tell you that they don't listen to the criticism, but I was listening and probably listening too much.

I became obsessed with the media. I would wake up and

comb through the local papers and even look for critics on the Internet. I watched the TV shows and kept a running tab of who was for me and who was against me. I knew where everyone stood: I knew that Mike Golic of ESPN thought that I should play if the doctors gave me clearance; I knew that John Dennis and Gerry Callahan, the morning guys at all-sports station WEEI in Boston, spent an entire show criticizing my comeback as selfish, egotistical, and life threatening.

One day I left the stadium and put on sports radio for my ride home. I shouldn't have done it, but I listened as callers and hosts talked about my decision to return. It was hard for me to take it, because they weren't commenting on my public job. If you want to criticize the way I play linebacker and say I suck, I can deal with that. But if you want to talk about the decisions I make in front of four people, if you want to question my wife and ask what she was thinking, that's where we are going to have problems. That type of criticism was affecting me a lot and it hurt. I had never been questioned as a husband and father, and it bothered me that people felt they had the right to do armchair quarterbacking in my household.

This personal decision was now watercooler talk. It got the attention of football fans as well as people who had no interest in the game. Depending on where you turned, I was either selfish and egotistical or courageous and inspirational. When Spaulding Rehabilitation Hospital had its thirty-fifth anniversary celebration, Heidi and I sat with Neil Sullivan and his wife, Jessica. Neil is a firefighter from Melrose, Massachusetts, who had to have his right leg amputated after it was crushed between two fire trucks in August 2005.

Jessica was aware of the criticism being directed at us, so she had some powerful words for Heidi. "I know what it's like to live through a tough situation, just like you guys do," she said. "A lot of the critics, the worst thing they've nursed their husbands and wives back from is a hangover." She made us laugh, and she wasn't done. "When you fell in love with him and married him, you took on all of his dreams, too."

I've always had a strong bond with Heidi, and all the events from February to October made it stronger. She was protective of me, and I of her. One day I marched into Stacey James's office, and he knew just how protective I could be. I had heard a rumor about an article that was extremely critical of Heidi.

"Try to find it," I said. "This is wrong. Find an article that's critical of Heidi and, I swear, I won't talk to anyone else in the media this season, or for the rest of my career."

It was a false rumor, but I had a decision to make. I was either going to futilely talk back to newspaper, radio, and TV critics who didn't understand what I was doing, or I was going to shut them out and concentrate on playing football. I needed to accept that everyone wasn't going to get it until they saw me make a tackle and get up from the pile in one piece. A lot of people thought I was going to die on the field, or they thought I'd be like Brian Mullen. Mullen played in the NHL for eleven years, including time with both New York teams, the Islanders and the Rangers. He had a stroke in 1993 and tried to come back, but he had a seizure a year later and his career was over. I didn't believe our situations were similar, but I understood the need for people to compare me to someone else because what I was doing was tough to grasp.

I think the whole period was a great test of my faith. I was raised Catholic and have always been diligent about saying my prayers. The stroke didn't intensify my faith, nor did it diminish it. But it did make me think about what God wanted from me in this situation. It made me wonder if it were meant for me to take on stroke and give hope to all stroke survivors.

I'm telling you, you have a stroke and it involves almost more emotional and mental healing than physical. You go to bed one way, and you're not like that when you wake up. It's tough on your mind. You're sort of ashamed of yourself because you had a stroke. That's how I felt in the beginning. I felt that something was wrong with me and there were hours at a time when I kept asking myself, "How could this have happened to me?" Maybe this sounds a little silly to say, but I was also embarrassed when I left the house. It was just weird at first that everyone knew what happened and that something was wrong. From what I understand, processing all the physical changes is especially tough on stroke survivors who are under forty years old. And there's a lot of them. I get letters from people saying, "My dad is still having problems dealing with having a stroke." That is a big part of the healing process.

Being a pioneer or a trailblazer wasn't my goal in the beginning. I was just trying to get my life back and be who I was, because the doctors said that was possible. It wasn't about orchestrating a media campaign or backing the Krafts into a corner. I didn't have time to think about a media campaign. I'm not addicted to fame, as one writer suggested. My focus was literally closer to home. Heidi would hold me up on the days that I was feeling emotionally weak, and there would be days I'd do the same for her.

"I can handle this," I told her. "If there's one guy who can do this, it's me."

I could feel things changing in my life. I could feel that this wasn't just my return to the field anymore. There were letter writers from New England and beyond who had put themselves in my shoes and were drawing inspiration from me. It was great to read what they had to say, especially during a time when the mainstream media response was not positive. These were stroke survivors, young and old. These were daughters and sons, husbands and wives, friends and colleagues. They didn't know me, but they would share a stroke-related story of their own and encourage me to keep going. Their encouragement gave me strength and confidence. It also meant that I was expected to have a broader scope when it came to discussing stroke. I was no longer representing myself, so there were times when I felt that I had an anonymous—and supportive—army at my back.

But there were days when I didn't have that confidence. There were days when I was trailed by self-doubt, days when I felt that I had taken on too much responsibility. The dynamics had changed, and that was cool when I wasn't thinking about it. But sometimes I'd step back and think how the course had taken a sudden turn. In the beginning, the plan was not to carry the dreams of stroke survivors, but that's what I had taken on. Without asking. I was a dream carrier. It's exciting when you are full of confidence, and it can overwhelm you when you're not.

And that's what happened to me as I sat in my kitchen one night and thought about what was in front of me. Each part of my life was being tested in 2005. It was a test of my marriage, my ability to make decisions with my wife, and my courage. This was a test of what I would do in a dire situation, a situation that is framed by uncertainty and the unknown.

"I can't fail," I said to Heidi that night.

She was confused. "What are you talking about?" she asked.

"There are too many people counting on me," I answered. "I just can't fail."

"What is failing, Tedy?"

"I don't know. But I know I can't fail because it would let too many people down. Failing is not playing well. Failing is going out there in the first game and looking like someone who had a stroke. Failing is having another stroke. Failing is dying."

I had been terrified to say those words: *failing is dying.* I said them slowly and quietly. It was the first time I had articulated the other side. When I play a football game, I always have to acknowledge the possibility that we could lose the game. This was the first time in months I thought of the post-stroke possibilities: another stroke, not being the same, dying. I had too much on my mind. I broke down, putting my head into my folded arms. Heidi stood behind me, rubbing my shoulders. She has told me many times that I take on a lot of pressure without letting it escape. I let it escape that night, and I'm glad I did.

We decided that the TVs were going to be turned off, the newspapers were going to be tucked away in a corner, and the radios would be tuned elsewhere. It was time for me to stop being a critic of the critics who talked about me in the media. It was time for me to take my anger and frustration to the place it's been taken since I was fourteen: the football field.

8

TAKE ME HOME

It was the first day of the unknown, and if I had really been analyzing it, I would have had the same combination of nerves and curiosity as everyone else. It was Wednesday, October 19, my first official practice of 2005. Reporters and cameras circled my locker, filming me as I pulled up my socks and filming me as I rubbed Tiger Balm on my knees. I remember the smell of menthol and cinnamon from the balm, and I remember cameras positioned at all angles. Everywhere I turned there was a camera. They wanted to film me sitting down, putting on my shells, and tying my shoes. Given all the commentary about my comeback, some of the reporters must have been wondering if they were covering a man who had a death wish.

It was a wild, circuslike scene. My locker room neighbor, Larry Izzo, was pushed out of his space because the overflow crowd huddled around my locker and also took up his.

While I didn't appreciate the majority of the opinions that were offered about me and my family, I had to keep reminding myself that this was a new story and a new topic to most people. They either didn't realize it or they chose to ignore that this was a process that Heidi and I had cried, argued, and rejoiced over since February. I understood the fears people had, because they were the same fears that we had before we were educated about stroke. But the next step was what bothered me, and I felt that it was a step across the line. I just had a problem with a family decision becoming a major topic in the media. In my opinion, they were different worlds.

As much as lashing out at someone might have crossed my mind, I knew I wasn't going to respond that way. An athlete never looks good in that situation, no matter what his reason is for going off on the media. More important, I wasn't going to bring a sideshow like that into the locker room. I was trying to fit in with my teammates again, and the best way to do that was to think about football, just like they were.

While I was working, I didn't think about the philosophical "should he or shouldn't he?" discussions that commentators were having about me. I didn't think about Dr. Greer giving me two words that most patients don't want to hear: no data. There was no data for a case like mine, because no one in professional football had ever had a stroke and come back to play again. Although I had been medically cleared and called neurologically normal, no one ever issued any guarantees. For example, when I asked about the possibility of the device in my heart moving, I was told that it *shouldn't*. I would have gone crazy if I had sat around wondering why it was *shouldn't* rather than *won't*.

My teammates and coaches realized I was going to be in a unique position for the rest of the season. There were going to be questions about returning after the stroke, and the questions wouldn't just be directed at me. Bill Belichick knew that the media would want to get analyses and reactions from him as well as from my teammates. Bill is good at handicapping where the media want to go and how they want to get there, so during a team meeting, before my first practice, he decided to take on the situation directly.

"There's going to be a lot of media interest in Tedy," the head coach said. "And I'm going to advise you all not to comment on his health. I haven't even commented myself. The only person who should be commenting on the health of Tedy is Tedy."

I can imagine that many of my teammates had questions and weren't exactly sure how or when to ask them. So if there was any talking about what I was capable of doing in that first practice, it wasn't coming from the team.

I didn't expect to be pounded on the back with "Attaboy"s when I slipped on my jersey and took the field. In another profession, maybe you're looking for a "Welcome Back" banner when you return to work after being away for eight months. For me, the welcome back was physical and abrupt: my first contact drill was a 9-on-7 in which I was supposed to knock heads with a fullback. But this was no ordinary fullback. Playing the role that day was Eric Alexander, who is actually a 240-pound linebacker. The 9-on-7 is a good contact drill, and the setup is as simple as it sounds. The offense has nine guys and the defense has seven, and they are trying to establish something that we're trying to take away. Generally, we know what they're going to do on offense and they know what we're going to do defensively.

Dean Pees, our linebackers coach at the time, was in charge of scripting the plays. Coach Pees didn't say anything to me before the practice, but he said all he needed to with his first call of the drill. He wanted a fullback lead, which is probably the most violent collision I can have on the field. The fullback runs at me and it's my job to stand him up, shed him, and then make the tackle. I was excited when the play began to unfold. I knew Eric's momentum was going to lead to a forceful hit when he reached me, and the speed I was generating would do the same. It was going to be my power versus his. My mind was as clear as it had been in weeks, and the only thing running through it was that it was good to be working again. The thought was brief, maybe a split second long, and then instinct took over. I hit Eric hard, hard enough that it seemed like there was a loud explosion in my helmet. It was a spectacular hit for both of us, helmets and pads coming together at about the same time. Neither of us fell to the ground, but Eric got a solid shot to my chest; it seemed as if the impact woke up my entire body.

It was going to be the first and last time that I would think about the device in my heart while I was on the field. After that sternum shot from Eric, I paused for a moment and thought, "Okay, I'm all right. I'm still here. Let's go."

The next play I took on Billy Yates, an offensive lineman with a big block head. Billy isn't much taller than I am, but his listed weight is 305 pounds. He just may be the strongest guy on the team. I hit him and didn't have any problems. Long after the drill was over, I glanced at Coach Pees, who had specifically called for this type of contact.

"Hey," he said with a hint of a smirk. "I'm just trying to get you ready for the games."

I was back in the NFL, but I wasn't back to normal for long. About forty-five minutes to an hour before my second practice, I had to take an unexpected trip to Massachusetts General Hospital. For some reason, infections were common in our locker room that year, and I had one on my right elbow. I thought it was a spider bite at first, but then it just kept swelling. It got to be the size of a pear, and it had already been drained once. It wasn't responding the way the training staff wanted, and no one knew why. One of my theories was that we used field turf for our practice field, and the synthetic grass locks in bacteria. On natural grass, the rain washes away everything. It was just my theory, though, and the training staff wanted answers that came from someone with more expertise.

"Do you want to run to Mass General real quick before practice?" Jim Whalen asked.

"Real quick?" I said. "It's going to have to be, because I don't want to miss this practice."

I couldn't miss practice on my second day back on the job. I thought of all the speculation that would take place if the media watched the first thirty minutes of practice and didn't see me there. *Did he have another stroke? What happened? Why isn't he here? I told you so.*

Dave Granito had the assignment of driving me to the hospital so we could see team doctor Bert Zarins. We jumped into

Dave's old Jeep and headed north for the thirty-mile trip to Boston. He was going as fast as he could, pushing 80 miles per hour, weaving in and out of traffic.

"Can't this thing go any faster?" I said to Dave.

"I can get you there at this pace," Dave said, "or I can go faster and we'll both be on the side of the road." He knew the Jeep better than I did, and he knew if he pushed it too much he might just flip it over.

We were going to be able to save five or ten minutes once we got there. Because my stroke led to a lot of media attention and speculation, Mass General went out of its way to ensure that my other trips there would be extremely private. For example, hospital security would be notified that I was on my way and would give us instructions on where to meet them, near a back entrance. Someone would park the car for me, I'd be taken on an elevator to my appointment, and when the appointment ended I'd be led back to the elevator and taken directly to my car. The same things happened as we were speeding through Boston traffic to see Dr. Zarins.

The doctor knew I was coming and knew exactly what to do. I lay on a table, put my left arm by my side, and the swollen area was cut into twice.

"Okay, Tedy," Dr. Zarins said. "You're all done."

I made it back to practice just in time. Bill is usually the last guy on the practice field, and I jogged right by him and smiled as he walked there. He knew the story of my trip to Boston, and I think he wound up delaying the start of practice a few minutes. As for the infection, we couldn't figure out if it was a bug bite or something in the dirt. It was a nonissue after a couple days.

The real challenge for me was to get my timing, conditioning, and strength to an acceptable level by October 30. That was the night of the seventh game of the season, the first time I would be eligible to play after beginning the year on the physically unable to perform list. By rule, I had to sit out the first six games of the season. Then there was a three-week window in which I was allowed to practice. If the team didn't activate me after those twenty-one days, I would have to miss the rest of the year. I knew I wasn't in danger of missing the season, but there were questions about whether I'd prove to be good enough to play a significant role against the Buffalo Bills on the 30th. My conditioning was fine, perhaps too fine, because my weight had dropped to about 235. I like to play in the 240s, so I cut down on my running in an attempt to retain more weight.

Practices were going as well as I could have expected, and as we moved toward the thirtieth, it started to become obvious that I was going to play against the Bills. At one point during the week, Coach Pees—a straightforward, no-nonsense type—even told me that I was going to start the game. I had guessed, incorrectly, that I would be worked into the rotation gradually. I was looking forward to the game, not just for me but also for our team. We were at the bottom of the league in several defensive categories, and we weren't close to forcing as many turnovers as we had in the previous two Super Bowl seasons. We don't like to use injuries as an excuse, but there was no denying that they affected us. We lost our top middle linebackers—Ted Johnson, Roman Phifer, and me—in just one off-season. Our secondary was unrecognizable, either due to injuries (Rodney Harrison), guys not playing their natural positions (Troy Brown), or departures to other teams (Ty Law). But I still looked at the Buffalo game as our opportunity to start a run. It was going to be our first divisional game of the year, and it was going to begin a stretch in which we would play four of six games at home after beginning the year with four of six on the road.

Officially, it was going to be Buffalo against New England. But I understood the significance of my return, and I knew that all eyes would be on me as I took the field. The local and national media began to get into position a few days before the game.

Since ESPN had the national telecast, several of the network's broadcasters and producers asked to set up an interview with Dr. Greer a couple days before the game. I talked with him about the request, and we agreed that he should honor it—with a couple of restrictions. The entire interview was going to be off the record, and there was going to be nothing specific about my stay in the hospital. Dr. Greer wanted to use the opportunity to educate the national media about all aspects of stroke: What is it? What does it do? What are some of the things neurologists do to work up a young stroke patient versus an older one?

I wasn't surprised when Dr. Greer gave a report of his conference call with the ESPN personalities and producers. He is a personality himself, so I knew he'd be able to entertain and educate as he talked with the likes of Joe Theismann, Mike Patrick, Paul Maguire, and several producers. He spent a few minutes asking the network not to bill the Buffalo game as some pre-Halloween freak show. He felt that too many in the media were painting a bleak picture of what was happening instead of seeing this story for the comeback that it was. As usual, Dr. Greer handled all the potentially awkward questions with humor and grace. But the doctor may have reached his educational—and jaw-dropping—peak when he was asked at the end of the interview if he was excited to watch the game against the Bills.

"Excited to watch it? I'm *not* going to watch it," he said. "It's a late game, I've been working fourteen- and fifteen-hour days, and I have a tough week ahead of me. I'm not staying up to watch a football game. I'll be in bed by nine."

Imagine the message it must have sent to those who still had doubts about my safety. Dr. Greer wasn't going to spend the night pacing in front of his television, wondering if something was going to happen to me on the field. He was confident that I was back to normal. And besides, as he reminded me several times, he's a Steelers fan.

On the Saturday night before the game, I joined the rest of my teammates at a local hotel. We always stay in hotels before games, whether we're at home or on the road. For me, one of the best things about meeting at the hotel was the seven o'clock meal I'd have with a few of the regulars. It would be the same group each time: Christian Fauria and Dan Klecko—who are now with other teams—along with Mike Vrabel and Larry Izzo. It was just our little moment to tell stories and relax, and we finished off the meal with some apple pie and ice cream. It was always fun to be around that crew, which provided the lighthearted warm-up act to the coaches' more business-oriented meetings and walk-throughs. After the meetings on Saturday the twenty-ninth, I remember being touched by an e-mail that was sent to my BlackBerry. It was from Terry Francona, the manager of the Red Sox and a fellow University of Arizona alum. It read,

"Congratulations on your comeback, your courage, and your perseverance." The last word stuck with me because I felt that it was perfect. Perseverance; I had never heard anyone describe it that way, but I thought it was appropriate. I called Heidi.

"That's what we've been doing this entire time, honey. We've been persevering," I said. "He got the right word. We've persevered through the stroke, the rehab, the decision to play, and the critics."

After talking with Heidi, I said prayers and read from my prayer book. I consider myself a good Catholic, and I was one before the stroke happened. The only difference is that my prayers now are a little different. I do spend more time giving thanks for life. I always try to take the attitude that every day of life, good or bad, is great. I may have gone through a frightening time with the stroke and all the questions and issues that came with it, but I wouldn't change a thing about it. I did have moments of weakness when I was mad at God and asked, "Why me?" But I understand that it was meant to happen to me. Why? I think I'm still learning some of the reasons.

As I paged through my prayer book the night before my first game of 2005, I saw Francona's word—"perseverance"—in there, too. I took it as a sign that I was meant to come back. It was a major word and major inspirational point for me as I thought about playing again.

I was refreshed, not nervous, when I woke up the next morning at the hotel. I may have had some anxiety if it had been a game at one or four in the afternoon. But since it was a night game, the last of the day, I had time to go home and spend time with my family before going to the stadium. Tony was in from

Las Vegas and, by chance, my in-laws were also in town. They had planned to visit earlier in the year, long before I thought of playing football in 2005. It was good enough for them that they had come in from Arizona to see us and their grandchildren, but now they were going to see a football game as well.

It was interesting to see my father-in-law, Bill Bomberger, at that time. When I was trying to decide whether to come back or not, I had a conversation with him. He asked, "What else do you have to prove? You have a beautiful wife, three kids, you've won Super Bowls, and made the Pro Bowl. What else?" At the time, when I was still weak-bodied and unfocused, he was right that there was nothing left to prove. But when I saw Bill on the day before Halloween, everything had changed, so much so that I said to myself, "I've got everything to prove now."

Once I decided that I was going to come back—and once I realized that stroke survivors were counting on me to come back—I had to do it. I had no choice. There was a weight of responsibility on me, and it was much different in October than it had been a couple months earlier. I didn't know how I would play, but I did know I was going to be out there. What changed was that the "we" of Heidi and me became the "we" of a stroke community—survivors and supporters—I didn't even know. I guess the same thing happens in sports when thousands of fans are counting on you to deliver in a game. Of course, the difference is that although we sometimes talk about sports as life and death, the result of a game does not determine whether I live or a fan of mine dies. Fighting stroke truly is a daily life-and-death struggle for many out there. I didn't understand how deep it was until after I played against the Bills and got some of the letters, but just my presence on the field changed lives and knocked down walls. People saw themselves when they saw me, a fact that continues to amaze me.

On the day of the game, I was able to relax at home for a few hours before facing the entire football nation. I played with the kids, had my pre-game meal of filet mignon, broccoli, and a baked potato, and talked with the family. I've never been one of those players who needs to go into game mode several hours before the game actually begins. I can easily flip the switch between dad and linebacker. So I was dad/husband/brother/ son-in-law until about four-thirty in the afternoon, when I decided to make the trip to the stadium.

As I drove, I thought about some of the things I had been asked during the week. It occurred to me that I hadn't been asked about the Bills' players one time. All the questions were about the stroke and the return. I gave the media what they wanted during the week, or at least I tried. But I didn't have the luxury of solely focusing on what this game meant for me when I knew that our team would be challenged to control players such as Eric Moulds and Willis McGahee. I was starting to think about some of my game responsibilities as I pulled into the stadium.

I must have been more ready to play than I realized, because I got to Gillette too early. I didn't have a lot to do before 6:45, when I was required to be at a short meeting where they take roll call. They want to make sure we're all there before we go into our pre-game rituals. I walked into that meeting and immediately saw a few of the coaches. They gave me a nod as I went to my seat in the back of the room, and then Eric Mangini, our defensive coordinator, came in and gave us the goals for the game. The meeting lasted about thirty seconds. It was matter-of-fact and businesslike, the opposite of the scenes playing out in the parking lots and stands.

After the meeting, I went to my locker and sat down. I took a deep breath, and reached for my iPod. The locker room was still quiet, not quite at the pre-game buzz stage yet. I was still at least an hour away from putting on my pads. I was listening to a song by Phil Collins called "Take Me Home." It's the live version, which is about eight minutes long. It was a song I was listening to a lot when I was working out, and there was something about the phrase "Take me home" that made it special to me. I would think of home as a football field. It was my home and I was just trying to get back to what I was doing and where I'm from. Playing football. Home.

My locker is next to a door, so I went through it with the volume turned up high. I just wanted to go for a light jog around the stadium before getting dressed and ready for the game. It was like there was a concert in my head. I pushed open another door, and I was in the bowels of the stadium, walking by security guards and bystanders who were in the hallways having conversations. I couldn't hear any of them as I walked by, on my way to a tunnel that would spill out behind our bench. Before I got to that tunnel, I looked to the left and saw the X-ray room and the X-ray technicians, who gave me the same kind of nod that the coaches had a few minutes earlier. I felt like I was in a video, in which everyone was just staring at me. It was the look of, "Oh, man. He's gonna do it. He's really gonna play." There were security guards, a few people I recognized, and some random people—all staring.

I got to the tunnel, with the music still blaring, and I was alone. Walking to the closed doors, I pushed them open, and there was a flood of lights. I felt that I hadn't seen the bright stadium and TV lights in years. As I walked up the stairs, there were fans leaning over saying something to me. I couldn't hear them, and I'm glad I couldn't because I didn't know what they were going to say. I didn't know if it would be, "Go get 'em, Bruschi" or "Tedy! Are you crazy? What about your wife and kids, Tedy?!" I didn't know, but I didn't want to hear it. I didn't know how any comment, even an encouraging one, would affect me.

I ran up and down the field a few times, just to get loose. It was early, so there weren't many people on the field. There are always a few coaches, players, reporters, and stadium personnel on the field at that time. I blocked them all out; I wasn't planning to talk with anyone for the next six or seven minutes. The crowd I heard was cheering—for Phil Collins. He sang the familiar lyrics, and I could hear his fans singing along with him. Right in front of me I saw some signs in the stands and a few mouths moving. It seemed as if all the mouths were moving in slow motion. Those scenes repeated themselves a few more times—Phil and his fans, the fans at Gillette, and pre-game sprints—and then my warm-up (along with the song) was over. I went back inside, and prepared for the next round of stretching and drills. It was just after seven, still about ninety minutes before game time.

Some of the routines seemed as normal as usual, and others made me feel like a tourist on my home turf. There were no problems as I sat in front of my locker, stretching on my own, and looking over the game plan one more time. There were no problems when I helped Willie McGinest with his shoulder pads and Don Davis helped me with mine. It was what we had always done; the Buffalo game was just a continuation of something that had started years earlier. I don't remember anyone making any special comments about the comeback. We were all waiting for the usual countdown: special teamers taking the field to warm up first, and then skill guys, followed by "early birds"—people who want to take the field early—and big guys. It was good to hear one of our assistant coaches, Pepper Johnson, yell out at 7:50, "Two minutes!" That would be when we took the field and began our stretching as a team. I didn't have my iPod with me this time, so I could hear the warm reception for the team and me. It was loud then, and it would be even louder for team introductions. But before that happened, things began to get confusing for me.

Once we stopped stretching, I kind of spaced on where the linebackers were supposed to warm up.

"Tedy! Over here." It was Mike Vrabel calling from the other side of the field where I was supposed to be. I ran over there, and I honestly didn't know what drill to do. It was the same one I had been doing for nine years, but I was suddenly a mess. I didn't think I was nervous, but something was making me forget drills that I used to be able to do without thinking. But on that night, Mike had to talk me through every one. It was funny because, as a captain, I was positioned at the front of the group. And I was a captain who didn't know what to do.

"This is the drill," Mike said. "You gotta hit and then you tackle. Remember?"

"Oh, okay," I'd say. "That's right."

We would do a 7-on-7 drill—a passing drill without offensive and defensive linemen—and then I'd start to run off again.

"Tedy! Over here. You're on punt team. You've got to warm up with the punt team."

Mike and special teams coach Brad Seely were laughing at me. I saw Mike and Brad talking, and I asked Mike later, "What did Brad say?" Mike answered, "Well, Brad said, 'Tedy doesn't know where the heck he is, does he?'" I laughed because he was right. I may have been in uniform at that moment, but I wasn't all there.

It was getting close to game time, and I was going to have to be a lot sharper than I was in warm-ups. As the captains from both teams approached midfield for the coin toss, I saw a familiar face and jersey number—36—coming toward me. It was my former teammate Lawyer Milloy, who was drafted by the Patriots the same year I was. Lawyer was released by the Patriots five days before the start of the 2003 season and quickly signed with Buffalo. When he heard about the stroke, he called early on to see how I was doing. Now he was walking toward me as a Buffalo captain, and I walked a little faster so I could meet up with him. We embraced, I thanked him for his support, and he told me it was good to see me back on the field.

And what a field it was. I thought it was spectacular when I jogged alone before the game, and I was even more impressed when I huddled with my teammates before we were all introduced. I waited with them all in the tunnel and told them how important it was for us to set the tone in this game. It was not the time for me to be mentioning anything about it being my first game back, because that was the secondary story for the team. As we broke our huddle, it took me a while to notice the very gracious and unselfish act that my teammates were doing for me. They quickly took the field before I did so that I could be the last player introduced. It was incredible: I heard my name followed by the loudest ovation of my professional career. It's a snapshot that still gives me chills when I think about it. I looked around the field that night and thought, "I can't remember seeing so many cameras for a regular-season game." I've played in enough big games to know how the atmosphere is different from a game during the season, and this Sunday-night matchup had the electricity of the playoffs. I could feel it as I ran on the field for the first play. I don't know if I was thinking too much during warm-ups, because I wasn't having any recognition issues when the game began.

I got a good idea of what the Bills wanted to do on the very first play of the game. It was no surprise: they gave the ball to their running back, Willis McGahee, and he gained 4 yards. This was not going to be an easy game for me. They wanted to run the ball, and they were probably going to be coming my way a lot. Their second play was more of the same: McGahee to the right for a yard. They clearly felt they could control the clock and run the ball against us. I was excited to be out there with my guys, against this team, in front of this crowd. I couldn't wait to get my hands on the ball or make some type of play that would signify that I was back.

On the Bills' third play, I noticed that number 11 for them, receiver Roscoe Parrish, was entering the game. Mike Vrabel, who was also playing inside linebacker, saw the same thing I did.

"Eleven's in, Tedy," he said. "Reverse alert." We both understand that every team has a "gadget" guy, a player who is a threat to throw from an unusual position—like Washington's Antwaan Randle El, a receiver who was a quarterback in college. If Parrish is in the game, the defense has to be ready for a reverse. That's exactly what happened. I was able to slow Parrish down behind the line of scrimmage, and Mike and Vince Wilfork were able to wrap him up for a 6-yard loss.

Another significant play in the first series was Buffalo's version of the power play. The idea is that they double-team one of our ends, and one of their guards is supposed to pull. My job as a middle linebacker is to scrape past that double-team and bounce the run outside to another linebacker. I slipped the block inside and went low because I saw the running back, Willis McGahee, coming. I made the tackle, which is not what made the play noteworthy. What stood out was that the tackle was my first "pile," the kind of play that ends with your teammates piled up on your back. It's something that most football players don't think twice about, but you might if you had a procedure in which a device was placed in your heart. But just as I had in practice after the stinging collision with Eric Alexander, I stood after the McGahee tackle and subsequent pile and knew that I was going to be all right. My thought was, "Get up quick. I've got three seconds to spring up, or Heidi is going to be nervous."

After a while, the fans weren't as concerned about me as they were about our defense. On the Bills' first two drives of the game, they had run a staggering twenty-four plays. They didn't get any points in the first quarter and managed just a field goal in the second, but they were killing us with their time of possession. On the sideline, I tried to make a point to our defense while also trying to lighten the tense mood.

"Fellas, the first drive was fourteen plays. The second drive was ten. This is my first game back. Can we get a three-and-out so I can get a rest?"

The cameras were on me, even when I was on the sidelines, and a cynical side of me felt they were there for a reason: to see me keel over and collapse. I do think there was an unspoken car-crash element to the coverage, as if this was going to be one of those gruesome accidents that you think you don't want to see but you look anyway. I remember gritting my teeth during the broadcast, with a camera a few feet away from me. I said to myself, "You're not going to get what you want out there. Not tonight. I'm not going to fail."

I looked in the stands a few times to see how Heidi was doing. She was sitting next to her father, and that put me at ease, because I wondered what kind of comments she might hear from some drunk fan. If anyone said anything, I was glad that her father would be there when I couldn't. I probably acknowledged her two or three times during the game by placing three fingers over my heart. Three was Heidi's volleyball number in college, so it was my way of communicating with her during games. She was a sign-language minor in college, with a major in special education and rehab, and she often gave me an "I love you" in sign language.

The cameras were on Heidi so much that she was getting calls on her cell phone. "You're on TV every ten seconds," one of her friends said. "Don't pick your nose or anything." She certainly wasn't picking her nose, but she was wearing a coat that was symbolic of how far we had come in eight months. Whenever the two of us would watch a TV story about the stroke, there would be footage of us walking out of the hospital. We got used to seeing the clip of me in gray sweats and Heidi in the black coat. That clip represented the low point for us, and Heidi would look at it and say, "I'm so tired of seeing that coat. I'm going to burn it." Instead of burning it, she tossed it in a closet. And as she rushed out of the house on the thirtieth, she reached for a coat that she might need just in case the unseasonably warm October night turned cool. It did, and she didn't think about how she grabbed the same black coat, but this time for something good.

Back on the field, we needed more than good karma. The Bills were running and passing well against our defense. We were doing a good job of keeping them out of the end zone when they got inside our 20-yard line, but they were coming away with points. They led 10–7 after three quarters and 16–7 with ten minutes left in the game. You could feel the frustration of the New England fans, and you could sense their focus changing as well. This was no longer the Tedy Bruschi Comeback Game. It was a game the Patriots had to win, and there was a nervousness setting in among the fans. I don't know if it's a product of all our success, but I never thought we were going to lose. I felt that someone was going to make a play, somehow, and we were going to pull the game out.

It took Tom Brady just a few seconds to ignite one of our biggest plays of the night, a 37-yard pass to Deion Branch. A few plays later, Corey Dillon scored from the 1 to make the score

16–14. But we still needed the ball and quickly. If the Bills could continue to run and grind out the clock, we were going to be facing a loss. All thoughts in the stadium changed, though, when Bills quarterback Kelly Holcomb was sacked by Rosevelt Colvin at his own 23-yard line. Rosey was able to jar the ball loose and recover the fumble, setting Tom and the offense up with great field position.

Just two plays later, we had the lead and the game, 21–16.

The box score said I finished with ten tackles, and ESPN even had a category for the number of times I was hit. I thought the "times hit" stat was funny: it's unheard of that a stat would be invented for one game. But what mattered to me was that people could see that this was not a horror show. Blood wasn't going to squirt from my helmet and I wasn't going to fall in a heap on the field. I wish ESPN could have sent cameras to different locations so they could have seen the variety of reactions to the game. One of their cameras would have shown—hilariously—Dr. Greer, confident and sound asleep. Another would have been focused on Anne McCarthy Jacobson, who was with me during my good and bad days of physical therapy. She couldn't keep her seat as she watched the game at home, so at times she stood nervously in front of the TV, waiting for me to get off the ground.

ESPN did have a camera on Mr. Kraft in the fourth quarter. He was being interviewed by Suzy Kolber, who asked him if he forced me to sign a waiver before I played. His response was thoughtful and kind: "Well, that's not the spirit of our relationship. I'm satisfied that he's made the right decision. Although I like lawyers, you can't let them run your life. Our relationship with Tedy Bruschi is not about signing releases and other things."

I didn't know it until I read my mail a week or two later, but it was also a huge moment for dreamers, fighters, survivors, and doctors. It was not a story of negligence; it was a night of inspiration.

In the locker room, we do something called a breakdown after a victory. We'll gather around at the center of the room, briefly talk about the game, and then sign off with a rhythmic "Aww, yeah." I usually do it. But Sunday, October 30, was an unusual day and night on many levels.

"I'm breaking it down today," someone said. It was Bill Belichick.

Everyone stared at him. Bill? We couldn't believe it. He led the call-and-response by asking, "I want to know how it feels to have Tedy Bruschi back." And everyone responded with the familiar "Aww, yeah." It was touching to me. Bill is not the most outwardly emotional person, but I thought that was cool. I gave him a hug and said, "Man, thanks. It could have used a little more rhythm, but it was good." He laughed, and I exhaled.

I was finally back. The first guy to come up to me individually was Tom.

"Congratulations," he said. "You're all heart, Tedy. All heart."

We hugged. I had been on the field for seventy-six plays in my first real game since the Super Bowl. "Man," Tom said. "You're going to be really sore tomorrow."

9

MY INSPIRATIONS

There's a great Eleanor Roosevelt quote that I now carry in my wallet. Heidi saw it first, and when she gave it to me I thought it was perfect because it applies to anyone who is facing any type of adversity: "You gain strength, courage and confidence by every experience in which you really stop to look fear in the face. You are able to say to yourself, 'I have lived through this horror. I can take the next thing that comes along.' You must do the thing you think you cannot do."

For me, looking fear in the face was returning to pro football when no one in my position had ever done it. Going through the decision-making process of whether to play or not after the stroke was the most pressure I've felt in my life. I was trying to get back to the field, but I knew that I wasn't making a football decision; I knew that if I made the wrong choice, the implications would be much greater than losing a game.

So for me and my family the unknown was resuming a football career after a stroke. For someone else it could be cancer, losing a parent, or losing a child. A *Boston Herald* columnist named Karen Guregian wrote about her Hodgkin's disease and said she better understood where I was coming from once she compared her situation to mine. No matter who you are and what you do for a living, there will be instances in your life when you'll have to show courage and be strong.

Since the stroke, I've heard from thousands of people of various ages, races, ethnicities, religions, and economic backgrounds, who have shared their stories with me. Some of them are current and former teammates and coaches, some are family friends, and some are complete strangers. They've all inspired me with their sincere visits, phone calls, text messages, e-mails, and handwritten notes.

Adam Vinatieri, my former teammate who now plays for the Indianapolis Colts, was kind enough to contact one of my favorite restaurants, Luciano's in Wrentham, Massachusetts. Adam called shortly after the stroke and told the staff there to take care of me, and the restaurant brought over a truckload of food. It was so much that we were able to feed the entire neighborhood. There were members of the local and national media who were gracious, too. Karen, Mike Dowling, Mike Lynch, Joe Amorosino, and Michele Tafoya were among many who sent food baskets and notes of encouragement. There's even a funny story about Tom Brady's sisters, Nancy and Julie. They were determined to do something nice for me following the stroke, so they made meatballs and pasta and even picked up fresh bread from a bakery. They personally delivered the food to me, working off of directions they printed from the Internet because they had never been to my house. It really was a sweet gesture—even if the meatballs were, well, not so sweet. I love Nancy and Julie to death, though. I remember that Tom sent me an e-mail saying, "Did you brave my sisters' meatballs?" Rosey Colvin brought over a blueberry pie from his wife, Tiffany. I had been asking Rosey about the pies—which are great—for a long time. When I see him now I say, "Do I have to have another stroke to get another pie?"

I could easily go on telling you about the profound messages that have been sent my way since February 2005. But to give you a better idea of what I went through, I'd like you to hear directly from some of the people who reached out to me. I'll begin with a note that touched me as much as it surprised me. It was hand-written in black ink, on sharp white paper. In the left-hand corner there was the familiar logo of the Dallas Cowboys, my favorite football team as a kid. The note was from my first NFL head coach, the legendary Bill Parcells:

Tedy,

I was saddened greatly to hear about your episode. I'll pray that you recover well and return to a normal healthy life with your wife and young children. These things can be shocking and disturbing when they happen. However, there is another side that happens when you return to what was before. I hope this happens for you as it did for me after a heart issue back in 1990.

I also wanted to commend you for a magnificent

career and what you and your team have accomplished. I knew when we drafted you we had a player, but even I didn't know how great you would become. You inspire a lot of people, myself included.

I hope and pray your future shines as brightly as your past. My thoughts are with you.

After I read the note, about a month after the stroke, I was struck by how far I had come. I may not have been doing well physically, but I had reached a point in my life where Bill Parcells was telling *me* that I inspired *him*, when it was just the opposite when I first came into the league. I was moved by Parcells's thoughtfulness. He's a busy man, and it meant a lot to me that he took the time to write. I only played a year for him, but we developed a good relationship during that season. I learned a lot from him.

One practice during my rookie year stands out. I was just learning to play linebacker, and I was showing signs that I might be able to play the position at a high level. Sometimes I'd make a few great plays in a row that would get the coaches' attention. After one practice at the old bubble facility in Foxboro— we would have to drive from practice to the stadium—Parcells called out to me. "Bruschi," he bellowed. "Come here. You're riding back with me." He drove a long Cadillac, an Eldorado that looked even more imposing when Parcells was behind the wheel. I had no idea why I was being singled out. Had I done something wrong? Had I been that bad in practice? I got into the car nervously. But for the next ten or fifteen minutes, Parcells simply talked to me about making smart decisions in my life.

"I just want to know if you're taking care of yourself," he said. "Are you saving money? Do you have an accountant?"

We didn't talk about the game itself during that time. Instead, Parcells lectured me about avoiding the traps that some players, rookies and veterans alike, fall into. He cautioned that there are players who have spent a number of years in the league but, because of unwise decisions, have nothing to show for it today. He wanted to be sure that I wasn't taking anything in the NFL for granted. I was blown away by the talk and impressed that the head coach had pulled me aside to focus on issues in my life. It showed me that he was concerned about more than breaking down the next opponent and telling me how to read a play better. It was something seemingly small, like the note he sent, but it was huge to me and something I'll never forget.

Parcells was not the only person with allegiances to another team who sent me a note. I received plenty of mail from Patriots fans, but I also heard from people around the country, even Raiders, Eagles, and Jets fans. Even before the stroke, I've always made it a point to read mail from the fans and respond when possible. It's important to me. The best fans of any team have a healthy respect for those of us who play the game, and I try to return that respect by showing them how much I appreciate their support.

I've been fortunate because I've been able to build friendships with some Patriots fans over the years. A fan from New Hampshire named Randy "Zip" Pierce has followed me every season of my career. I call him my number one non–family member fan. He doesn't let anything get in the way of his devotion to the Patriots. He was diagnosed with a rare optic nerve disorder in

1989 and was declared legally blind. About ten years later he lost his sight completely. But he still comes to the games. Zip also started making a "Bruschi Brew" up in New Hampshire. When he heard that I had stopped drinking, he switched the brew to root beer. I always go to his section after the games. Once, after getting to the stadium a little earlier than usual, I even stopped by his tailgating party to say hello to him and his friends.

I've always been treated well by the fans, but their response to the stroke was overwhelming. They were thoughtful and kind, and some of their statements reinforced just how deeply a professional athlete can affect people—especially kids—as a role model. Here's one example from a man named Bob who lives in Ohio:

Mr. Bruschi,

My family's prayers are with you and your family. I watched Super Bowl 39 with my wife and three sons. We laughed when your sons were chasing you during the "pre-game show." After the coin toss at midfield, you shook the hand of a young fan who was on the field and thanked him. I told my wife, "Now there's a class act." It seemed this year we had to be careful about allowing our kids to watch games with the antics going on. It was nice seeing the season end with your example of how men are supposed to play the game.

My oldest son is 13 and played school football for the first time this past year. His season finished and we watched some games together as the pro season wrapped up. He follows the Packers, so we were watching the Packers-Vikings game when Randy Moss fake-mooned the crowd. It wasn't something I wanted my son watching as he formed his opinions about football and what it's supposed to be. As we watched the Super Bowl, he pointed to you and said, "That guy's pretty cool."

Toward the end of the game, he asked, "Dad, what number were you when you played?" I wore 54. I told him that and he said, "54 is cool. I'm going to trade in my 72 for 54 next year."

Tedy, my son asked me a while ago how you were doing. All I know is what I hear on the news, but I told him that they said you were going to be all right. He said he was glad to hear it because you're a good player who likes kids. Number 54 certainly made a good impression on him.

Thank you.

Bob

I thought it was a good letter as well as a great example of how kids respond to our actions. I'm not saying that I don't like celebrations in the NFL, because I think a lot of them are just fun. Chad Johnson and the little Riverdance he does, that's fun. It's a form of expression, and I don't see anything wrong with it. But I do have a problem with doing something that will make a parent put his or her hands over a child's eyes because an athlete is acting like a fool. We're affecting a kid's growth. When we act like fools, we're giving kids something that they'll remember and interpret as the way things are supposed to be done. I'm not going to take it to the extreme and say we should censor people. I'm sure there's a clip of me out there using poor judgment, but that's in the flow and heat of the game. I understand that you have to be expressive and emotional. Just think about what you're doing and who could be watching.

Ironically, Randy Moss is now my teammate. People are always curious about what happens when a controversial player joins the Patriots. I tell them that we treat new guys the same, whether their reputation is good or bad. Our philosophy is that you begin to be judged based on your performance with the Patriots. It doesn't matter what you did anywhere else. Other new players are held to that standard; it will be no different for Randy.

Here's another letter from someone who is not a typical fan:

Hey Tedy,

Look, I'm a 48-year-old man. I don't send e-mails to athletes, don't wait in line asking for autographs, don't do any of those sports things. But you, Tedy, are an inspiration to all Americans. I hope you understand and know this. Football? Heck, it's a game. . . . But you are an icon here in New England. You're a great human being. I hope you realize that most folks, who wouldn't normally write to any athlete, think of you as a true mentor and example to our children, nieces and nephews—and reinforcement to us.

Now, you get your butt out of that goddang hospital, OK? You're a close friend to many more people than you could possibly think.

Andy

There were letters similar to Andy's and Bob's. There was one that made me laugh because the writer, a recent college graduate from Portland State University in Oregon, was multitasking me: he wished me good health, told me about his mother who had some medical issues, and concluded the note by asking if I needed an accountant. There was a fan of the Eagles, the team we had just defeated in the Super Bowl, who wrote, "Hey, Tedy. We're not done with you yet. We want another shot. February 5, 2006. Be there and be healthy. God bless you." Many fans said I was in their prayers, and while some of the writers were Catholics like me, I also heard from people of various religious beliefs. There was one man who didn't have to say he was praying; the entirety of his note was the Lord's Prayer.

I was seeing a new dimension of fan support. You can usually predict what the fan reaction will be when you win games and, ultimately, championships. But I didn't know what to expect to hear or read after the stroke. There were several themes and tones to the notes I received, but I feel comfortable calling them all educational. I was able to see how differently people approach situations that they consider to be crises. It obviously wasn't my plan, but it was as if I were taking monthly polls of average Americans. In the days and weeks after the stroke, most people who wrote encouraged me to be resilient and to take on stroke because my life was not over. As the Buffalo game got closer and stories of my comeback became public, some fans began to have the same hesitancy as members of the media.

What I heard most often in September and October was some version of this: "Tedy, you've done so much already. You have a beautiful wife and young children. Why not pack it up and walk away?" I understood that sentiment, and it was actually something I had heard from some of my own friends and family. But I also understood the sentiment of the Eleanor Roosevelt quote, and not only did I understand it, I lived by it.

Until you're faced with a frightening situation, you have no idea how you'll analyze it and get through it. After reading all of my letters, especially from stroke survivors, I felt that I had to dig deep for all the courage I had. In a way, I had no choice; I had to come back. One thing I learned from reading my letters is that there is a subtle difference between inspiration and pressure. At one point, I read all the words and felt more pressured than inspired. That's around the time I broke down in my kitchen and told Heidi, "I cannot fail." I was thinking of the letter writers and all the powerful things they had to say. I was their inspiration, but I allowed myself to wonder if they would be uninspired if I failed. Would I be delivering these people a setback if I didn't succeed at what I was trying to do? But I think the process of reading the letters over and over, and just accepting that I was in a public position to help people, helped me. I had to accept the responsibility of being an inspiration to people. Imagine if I had said, "I wish all these people could get inspiration from themselves because I can't take it." I had no desire to dismiss them, and, just as important, I had no right to.

I know this might sound crazy to some people, given the consequences involved, but I had to try. I didn't want to be mentally punishing myself five or ten years from now by saying, "You didn't even try." Of course, the other side of the argument is that trying—especially if something goes wrong—might prevent me from being the same man in five years. Or prevent me from being around at all.

I don't believe that life should be lived through a series of what-ifs. You have to be smart and cautious, but after you've educated yourself on whatever it is that you fear, you can't live a timid life, afraid of what might be hiding around the corner. You have to show courage, even before something chaotic happens in your life. There were many times I would "say" exactly that to my critics. I said it when I was at home, talking back to the critics in print, and on TV and radio. My talkback question to them is the same one I want to ask readers of this book: What would you have done? Would you have looked fear in the face and gone forward?

Shortly after the game against Buffalo, I went into my home office to read some of my mail postmarked late October and early November. While I didn't want to read or hear the comments on the day of the game as I listened to "Take Me Home," I did want to see what people had to say after they knew that I had made it. I sorted through dozens of letters before discovering an interesting contrast from the same family in Holliston, Massachusetts. A mother and daughter wrote me, separately, and I was struck by the transformation I saw in the daughter's letter. And although the daughter is a physical therapist who has worked with young stroke survivors, she didn't believe I could play football again until she saw stroke affect her own mother.

The contrast is fascinating on many levels. I'll start with Diane, who is the mother:

Dear Tedy,

I want you to know that you're an inspiration to me, a 53-year-old fan. You have long been a favorite of mine, both on and off the field. I was so touched by the clip showing two of your sons chasing you on the field before the Super Bowl. When you suffered your stroke I was very shocked and concerned, so I followed your recovery and progress with great interest. On September 8th, when I attended the Patriots' opening game, it was wonderful to see you looking so fit, even if on the sidelines. I never dreamed that only 10 days later, I would share your February experience.

Very ironically, on September 18th—while walking to the Panthers' stadium in Charlotte for the Patriots game—I became weak, started dragging one leg, and began slurring my speech. My husband, wearing your number 54 jersey, recognized my stroke symptoms. He rushed me to the Carolinas Medical Center where, after the initial assessment, the chief of neurology thought that I had a PFO. In fact, he said, "It's what Tedy Bruschi had." All of my symptoms resolved in 70 minutes and I had no residual deficits. In this regard, I was more fortunate than you.

After being started on Coumadin, I flew home to Massachusetts to make treatment decisions. The myriad of appointments led us to conclude that I needed minimally invasive surgery to close the hole in my heart.

So, as I face surgery next week at the Deaconess, I take heart in the fact that you overcame great obstacles to excel once again in a contact sport. That encourages me as I face my recovery and return to work as a hospital pharmacist—although friends and family joke that I'll be able to play football like you.

I loved Diane's letter, for many reasons. I liked that she and her husband were able to quickly recognize the stroke symptoms and get to the hospital. Because they acted with such urgency, Diane could have been within the time to be administered TPA, the clot-busting drug that can be given in the first three hours of an ischemic stroke. I was also glad to hear, from Diane and others, that the unexpected blow of a mild stroke is sometimes softened when a doctor says, "Tedy Bruschi had the same thing." There is a lot of stroke education out there, particularly from the American Stroke Association, but I wasn't aware of much of it until stroke hit me. Anything or anyone that brings stroke awareness to the mainstream is positive.

As you'll see from Diane's daughter, Cheryl, everything changes once stroke becomes personal. When it hits you or a member of your family, previous opinions can be reversed.

Tedy,

My prayers are with you and your family. I remember when I first heard that you had suffered a mild stroke. I couldn't believe it. I am a physical therapist and I've had a few young patients who have had a stroke, so I know that it happens. But for some reason I just couldn't believe that it happened to an elite athlete like you. . . .

When I heard about your stroke, I thought as a therapist, "I hope he never plays again," although as a fan I really wanted to see you back on the field. After seeing the video of you leaving Mass General, my fears were realized. To most people you probably looked all right, however I immediately began analyzing your gait and how off balance you looked. I figured there was no way you could play football again. . . . Hang it up and enjoy your family.

Your story hit home with me this fall. My parents were in Charlotte to see the Panthers and Patriots when my mom suffered a stroke. It affected her right side and her speech, but fortunately she had no residual effects. When she called to tell me about it her first words were, "I'm just like Bruschi." So now as a physical therapist and daughter, my perspective has changed. I did lots of research to find out everything I could about PFOs. My mom is going to have surgery this coming Monday at the Deaconess to repair the hole. I know that while it is still a very scary situation, my mom is able to find comfort in the fact that you had the surgery and you made it all the way back.

It gives her and me confidence that everything will be OK. I know she has a million questions which probably don't have answers, but seeing you play again on Sunday night was a huge relief. After learning more about what caused your stroke and my mom's stroke, I can honestly say that I think you and your doctors made the right decision. The surgery seems like it is a good answer to a correctable problem.

Watching you return to "full tilt, full time" is very comforting. My mom and I will be watching you guys on Monday night after her surgery, knowing that if you can do it so can she. Thank you for being an inspiration.

Do you know what I enjoyed most about Cheryl's letter? There was a transformation that took place in it. She was skeptical initially, just like a lot of other people. Her perspective changed when stroke affected her family. And I give her a lot of credit for doing her research and putting in the work to find out answers. I wish that some of the doubters in the media had done some of the same research and come to the same conclusion that Cheryl did. I hope this experience helps her in her job. Now when she sees a thirty-year-old stroke survivor, I hope she helps them see that they can overcome some obstacles that may seem impossible to scale.

I mentioned that Cheryl had a transformation in her letter, but I had a transformation—or a revelation—myself a few weeks later. That's when I met a physically small woman—she weighs less than a hundred pounds—with a big heart and an infinite amount of courage. Her name is Trisha Meili, but in April 1989 when her shocking story generated international headlines, she was known simply as the Central Park Jogger.

I was a couple months away from my sixteenth birthday

when Trisha's life changed forever, so I wasn't keeping up with current events as I do now. Trisha's story made newspaper columnists in this country wonder what was becoming of American society, and I can see why. One night while jogging in New York City's Central Park, Trisha was raped and brutally beaten by a group of teenagers who had decided to harass and bludgeon several strangers for "fun." Trisha was later found in the park with her hands tied and her body convulsing. In her book, *I Am the Central Park Jogger: A Story of Hope and Possibility*, she relayed stories of how the beating left her face looking like a Halloween mask. Because of the savage beating, she lost 75 percent of her blood and had a fractured skull. At one point she was administered last rites.

I was in awe at an event in Boston when this amazing woman, who was the keynote speaker, stood before me. Clearly, she was physically and mentally one of the strongest people I had ever met. She had been comatose in her New York City hospital room sixteen years earlier, and now she was delivering an enthusiastic and intelligent message about acceptance and hope. The young men who beat Trisha permanently altered the path of a highly educated (Wellesley and Yale), highly successful (investment banker on Wall Street) woman on the rise. But that wasn't the focus of her speech. She wanted to talk about going forward and dealing with whatever your current circumstance might be. If you're not the same as you were before, and in a lot of ways she isn't, what are you going to do? Are you going to try to retrace the exact life that you had, even if that's not practical? Or are you going to adjust to what lies before you?

When Trisha presented it that way, I leaned over to Heidi and said, "She's great. I've never looked at it this way before." Trisha doesn't remember the details of that awful night in the park, and maybe that's God's way of helping her. I can't imagine what mental torture that would be, continuing to relive and dream about that night.

Her situation was far worse than mine, but she made something in me click. She challenged me to consider and appreciate the question, What if things weren't the same? I can walk and I can see now, but I was lucky. The majority of stroke survivors have to adapt to changes stroke has made in their lives. I'm the best-case scenario; I'm extremely lucky.

Trisha helped remind me that when I'm with stroke survivors, I have to realize that most of their lives will be changed, and dealing with the change is the battle. With Spaulding, I was in front of stroke survivors who couldn't use their arms anymore or their speech was slurred. They were in a wheelchair because they couldn't walk. That's what they have to deal with in their lives, because sometimes it gets better but often it doesn't. So the tricky part is getting people to understand that who they are now—not who they were or hope to be—is okay. If you had a stroke and have deficits, it's all right. It's what you make of life afterward. For Trisha, that means being one of the best motivational speakers in the country, the author of a *New York Times* best-seller, and an interviewee of everyone from Katie Couric to Larry King. She still runs marathons, but she is not completely the woman she used to be, and she talks and writes about that.

After Trisha gave her dynamic speech, she met with a number of people, including Heidi and me. Later, she sent us a copy of her book. She signed it, "To Heidi and Tedy. You are a wonderful couple whose loving spirit touches so many. All of the best, Trisha Meili." Once I started reading the book, I couldn't put it down. If anyone ever asks me who inspires me, I'll tell them that Trisha has to be on the list.

The message from Trisha remains thoughtful and provocative. After thinking about it—and this is easy to say now—I think things would have been okay if my vision hadn't returned and my career had ended. Heidi would still be there. I'd still have my kids. I'd be able to watch them grow up and even be active enough to wrestle them to the ground on occasion, just like we do now. Maybe I wouldn't be able to drive anymore, but I think I would realize just how blessed I was to be alive.

I've received letters from stroke survivors whose spouses have left them, yet they still say in print, "The stroke was too much for my wife to take, but I still have my kids." It's shocking for me to hear it and read it, because I know that's something that never crossed Heidi's mind, not even for a second. You could say that she was the captain of my support team. And I had to learn to accept that support from her and everyone else who offered it. Sometimes pride and being strong-willed can prevent real support from taking place. When you need help, you have to be humble enough to accept it.

I remember reading about Ray Rhodes, a coach for the Seattle Seahawks, who had a stroke. He said he was stubborn at first and wanted to do everything on his own. He felt that using things such as a cane and a wheelchair took away his manhood.

I understood what he was saying, because I kind of felt the same way when I was leaving the hospital. But you have to reach a point where you understand that people who love you are just trying to help. I knew, for example, that I needed a wheelchair when I was being discharged from the hospital. If I didn't have it, I would have fallen on my face. So I didn't fight the fact that I had a problem walking.

There are random moments now when I'll be driving and think of the events that led to my return to the field. I'll think of the stroke, the rehab, the meetings with doctors, the critics, the letters, and my own changes of heart. I'll be thinking of those things in my car and I'll just get excited and say, "Yes, I pushed through. I had the toughest moment of my life, and I pushed through."

RETURNING

Officially, my return to the NFL happened on a warm Sunday night in October. Nearly 70,000 people saw it in person, and millions more watched in prime time on ESPN. The league even gave me a "Welcome Back" card, in the form of a Defensive Player of the Week Award. I played all right against Buffalo, accumulating 10 tackles, but I think the award was the NFL's way of acknowledging everything I had been through since I played my last game in February.

But those were just the official details of my comeback. Even though I was obviously on the field for the win against the Bills, I still didn't have the mentality that I needed as a football player. I was rusty and winded in the Buffalo game, and I could feel my legs weakening in the third and fourth quarters. Pursuing plays was taking a lot more effort than usual, and that's something I expected in my first game. What surprised me a bit was my reaction after we lost to Indianapolis the next week on *Monday Night Football.*

There is always a lot of hype when we play the Colts, and this game was no different. They were undefeated at 7–0 when they came to Foxboro, and the major pre-game question was focused on Peyton Manning: could he win in New England for the first time in his career? Manning had been a part of seven Colts-Patriots games in Foxboro and lost them all. He was incredible in game eight. He threw for 321 yards and 3 touchdowns. The Colts won, 40–21, and they were so dominant offensively that they didn't punt until the final two minutes of the game. Their coach, Tony Dungy, was extremely gracious when he approached me on the field. He told me that he was glad to see that I was back and that he was praying for me. I really appreciated the gesture from Dungy as well as other players and coaches around the league who went out of their way to seek me out and offer words of encouragement.

Even though the Colts kicked our butts, I wasn't as down as I usually am after losses. The problem was that I was seeing the big picture. If I didn't play pro football, maybe a philosophical approach about where I had been and how far I had come medically would have been a good thing. But you don't have that luxury if you want to play middle linebacker and be great at it and win championships. It didn't quite hit me at the time when I said it, but I didn't sound anything like myself when I talked to Heidi after the Colts loss. When I walked toward her, I noticed that she had what I call her "consoling face." Even after our wins, Heidi understands that part of me is there talking with her and part of me is replaying the game, trying to pinpoint what

I could have done better. So since this was a 19-point loss on national television, Heidi expected me to be dragging a bit.

"You know what, Heid?" I said to her. "I'm not going to be down about this because every time I walk off that field it's a victory."

She was proud of me for saying that. As much as I talked about returning to the job I had done before, I wasn't returning to it as the same old Bruschi; I was coming back as a stroke survivor. Honestly—and I know now that it was subconscious—I was thinking too much about that and other things. There are a couple reasons I was in that position.

Every two weeks I would go to Mass General for a "bubble test," technically known as the bubble study during an echocardiogram. By this point, I could easily recite the step-by-step process of the test: Tiny bubbles are created by agitating saline water, and then those bubbles are injected into a vein. Then the doctors watch the echo to see if they can see bubbles passing between the upper chambers of my heart. If they can, that could mean there's a PFO. I was working with Dr. Greer and Dr. Danita Sanborn, and they wanted to see if any on-field collision had affected the device that was now a part of my heart. They assured me that nothing would happen, and based on what they had already done for me, I had no reason to doubt them. But I couldn't help thinking that no one else had played football with this device, so I couldn't call the last guy this happened to and get his insight. It was happening to me, and I was establishing the precedent as we went along. It was unsettling for me each time I made that trip to Boston, especially after the first test, which took place after the loss to the Colts. I would make the drive to Boston and think to myself, "If they see a few bubbles, my career could be over. Just like that. Maybe something on the field has caused the device to dislodge, and that means my career is done." It was on my mind a lot. Once before a test I remember thinking, "These bubbles have so much power." Drs. Greer and Sanborn had a lot more confidence than I did at that point, and they were right. But all those tests, especially the first couple, were stressful.

On a different level, some of the media conversations I was having about the stroke were bringing stress, too. I felt that it was important to talk about it, encourage people to research it, raise stroke awareness, and help people recognize some of the warning signs. I still believe that it should be talked about and publicized, and that's one of the many reasons I continue to do work on behalf of the American Stroke Association. When I talked to the ESPN crew about my stroke, I had the sense that they were genuinely interested in hearing what had happened to me and what I had learned—and continue to learn—from it. Later, I talked with Steve Sabol of NFL Films for about forty-five minutes. I've always had a lot of admiration for what they do there, so while I rejected a lot of national requests at the time, I gave the okay to NFL Films. I also agreed to sit down with Andrea Kremer—a great reporter whom I've gotten along with for a long time—for about an hour, and that eventually turned into a three-part special on ESPN. As I said, I was happy to get the word out. But I felt that each time I talked about it, especially at length, I would get emotional and relive what happened to me. I finally told Stacey James that I couldn't talk about it anymore in production meetings before the game, because it was interfering with my preparation and mind-set. My plan was to concentrate on football in the short term and do the interviews with Steve and Andrea on back-to-back days around Thanksgiving.

I think that was the same time I went to Heidi and amended those words I said to her after we lost to the Colts. "Remember what I told you after that Indy game?" I asked. "Forget that. I want to win. It's a great victory to be back on the field, but I also want to beat people's butts, too." I wanted to make it clear that it was time to be a football player again, without holding back and looking for victories off the field. I knew I wanted to win and I was passionate about making it happen.

That was the transformation for me. We had split two games since I returned, and that was in step with how we had performed for most of the season; our record was 4–4. It was obvious that we weren't going to be at full strength for the rest of the season due to some of our injury problems. We had a lot of new players in the secondary, and they were going to have to be coached up fast. One of the great things about playing for Bill Belichick is that when he's analyzing the team, he calls out everyone, coaches included. He knew that the players and coaches would have to perform better over the final eight games of the season, and he actually said that in front of the team. I knew I had to get better and the team had to be better for us to have any shot at winning our third consecutive Super Bowl. No one on our team ever talked publicly about winning the Super Bowl, but the thought of three in a row was on my mind. I had so much respect and love for my teammates that I wanted to be part of something historic with them. The previous season, during the Super Bowl XXXIX run, I was so consumed with the dynasty concept that it even influenced some of the accessories I wore. Once I was in a Providence mall and I saw a pair of cuff links that caught my eye. I asked the salesperson about the distinctive design, and I was told that it was the likeness of Romulus and Remus, the mythical founders of Rome. Of course, I bought the cuff links and quietly reminded myself that they were appropriate because Rome was a formidable empire and we were trying to become a formidable NFL dynasty. (I did some research on Romulus and Remus later and found that the story wasn't all that nice: the twin brothers fought over which one of them was more favored by the gods, and the deadly dispute was settled when Romulus killed his brother.)

At the halfway point in 2005, the closest opponents to us in our division were the 3–5 Miami Dolphins. We didn't have a lot of time to sulk over our embarrassing loss to the Colts because we were going to have to face the Dolphins in Miami, where they always give us a competitive game. I went into that game with no restraint, no fear, and no big-picture perspective. I just wanted to win and get back to being a playmaking linebacker.

There was one play in the Dolphins game that confirmed that I was close to becoming the player I had been before. I was blitzing the "B" gap, which is the area between the guard and the tackle. The area widened, and suddenly Miami running back Sammy Morris stepped into the space to block me and protect quarterback Gus Frerotte. There was only one place to go, and that was through the air. I jumped over Sammy, intent on making a play. He hit me as I jumped, sending me spiraling through the air. I didn't care, because I've made plays that way before. As I was above the ground, I quickly thought of what I was going to do once I hit the grass. I thought, "Roll with it, and Frerotte will be right there." I did just that and took a shot at him with my right arm, grazed his leg, and just missed.

I didn't get to Frerotte on that play, but I felt good out there. It was easily my best game of the first three, even if I was credited with just four tackles. I was able to get my hands on the ball, and there was one play where I had middle-drop responsibility and knocked the ball down to prevent a Wes Welker touchdown. I was able to bat down another ball, and all I saw in front of me was a big old green field. I really did think I was going to score, but I was satisfied that all the things that Dr. Greer couldn't predict—playmaking ability—seemed to be within my grasp. I was satisfied with my play, my approach to the game, and ultimately the final score. We won, 23–16, although we didn't leave South Florida without some negatives. We allowed Frerotte to pass for 360 yards, the highest total he had thrown for in five years. And more important, we lost our starting center, Dan Koppen, to an injury that would end his season.

While the winning continued the following week with a 24–17 win over the New Orleans Saints, there was sadness in the locker room after the game. The players didn't know it during the game, but we found out later that Bill's eighty-six-year-old father, Steve Belichick, had passed away. Those of us who were on the team when Bill took over as head coach in 2000 were used to seeing his father at training camps, regular-season games, and Super Bowls. I remember late in Super Bowl XXXIX, when I was raising a celebratory bucket of water to dump on Bill and his father, I was thinking, "Should I do this? He is pretty old." And then I did it anyway, because it was a great moment between a father and son. I remember that Steve used to watch practices and games and get knocked down sometimes; some receiver would run out of bounds and knock Bill's dad down. There was one game when one of my former teammates, Otis Smith, bowled him over. Bill's dad was great; he would pop right back up and say, "I'm tougher than any of you guys." Every team needs that—the old-school guy who is tough and believes he can kick all of your butts.

When Bill told us about his father, a lot of players went up to him and said a few words and expressed their sympathies. I gave Bill a hug and told him I was sorry to hear the news. He thanked me and said, "I always knew my dad was tough—he was tough enough to deal with that ice water you dumped on us at the Super Bowl." Mr. Kraft gave Bill the game ball from the Saints win—Bill said he was coaching, understandably, with "a heavy heart"—and then Bill said he was off to Annapolis to handle some family business. Dante Scarnecchia, an assistant coach who has held every football job imaginable in Foxboro, led the team for two days while Bill was gone.

It was just before Thanksgiving, and we had won six of ten games. I had no illusions about our team: I thought that if we played well, there wasn't a team that we should fear. But on the flip side, since we weren't playing with all of our top performers on both sides of the ball, and especially in the secondary, reaching a high performance level would be tougher than it had been in the past. There was no Rodney, no Tyrone Poole, no Randall Gay. On offense, we were missing both Koppen and starting left tackle Matt Light. We had some injuries at running back with Corey Dillon, Kevin Faulk, and Patrick Pass. Going into a road game at Kansas City, our defense was not putting together great numbers. We were allowing several big plays each game, and teams were getting used to putting up 400-plus total yards against us. The only team that hadn't since my return was Buffalo, and the Bills still finished with 394. Still, with so many depressing stats against us, we were confident against the Chiefs. After we played that game, I'm sure several of our most loyal fans concluded that it wasn't going to be a championship season in New England.

We fell behind the Chiefs in the third quarter, 26–3. For a while, there was the hint of a comeback, but it wasn't enough to scare the enthusiastic, red-clad Kansas City fans in Arrowhead Stadium. The final score was 26–16, and, once again, an opposing offense was able to put up over 400 yards on us: the Chiefs finished with 420. It wasn't talked about much in New England, maybe because a lot of media people either didn't know about it or weren't sure who the speaker was, but one of the most significant monologues in Kansas City occurred at halftime. We were already down 19–3, and we had allowed Larry Johnson to rush for 79 of his 119 yards. The Chiefs were pushing our defense off the ball, and their aggressive defense harassed, hurried, and forced our offense into multiple turnovers. It wasn't surprising that someone in our locker room was going to have something to say about it. The surprise was the speaker: linebackers coach Dean Pees.

Coach Pees is the last person you would expect to tear into us with animation and profanity. It was his first season with the team, and he was still a work in progress with us when it came to "hard" coaching. He is a coach who has the players' respect because of his wisdom and matter-of-fact teaching method. He is usually not a screamer, although he was very clear in letting us know that he was ashamed that we had played so poorly in the first half. He said he came to New England because he wanted the opportunity to coach some special players, and that we were letting him down. Guys joke about it now because he used a phrase that day that most of us had never heard: "Burr up." As in, "It's time for you all to burr up and play football." We didn't laugh then, but to this day you'll hear someone in the halls making a reference to "Burr up." For those who viewed the Kansas City game from afar, it was a total disaster. For those of us who were in the room and heard Pees speak, it was a spark that wasn't going to necessarily stop with a strong second-half showing in Kansas City. Maybe, despite our 6–5 record, we still had a chance to go on a run.

Bill isn't shy about calling out specific players on our team to make a larger point, so I became one of his targets as we prepared for our twelfth game of the season, a divisional game against the New York Jets. "You know what I'm tired of?" Bill asked at a team meeting. "I'm tired of all the feel-good stories about the Patriots. Bruschi is a part of it, and I guess I'm a part of it, too. Do you know what would be a great feel-good story? If we go out on Sunday and beat the Jets."

I knew what feel-good stories he was referring to. There were many stories about Bill's resiliency and resolve to coach as he dealt with the loss of his father. And of course there were the stories about me and the stroke. As I sat there in the team meeting, a half-smile appeared on my face. I had given a lot of interviews and said a lot of things, and now it was being thrown back in my face. But I agreed with Bill; I was as tired of the feel-good stuff as he was. I just wanted to get back to being a football player, but I was going to have to deal with various networks showing interviews that I had recorded earlier. The great news for me was that the twice-monthly echocardiograms were not causing the stress that they had the first week in November. Drs. Greer and Sanborn had told me many times that the device that had been surgically placed in my heart was now a part of my heart and was not going to move. I finally got to a point where I could hear and trust their words and not think that my career was going to end with the next appointment.

On the field, we couldn't have fulfilled Bill's words more perfectly. Granted, we were facing a Jets team that was 2–9, had dropped six consecutive games, and had lost its top two quarterbacks to injury and was left with Brooks Bollinger calling the plays. But with the generous chunks of yardage we had allowed during the season, we couldn't be arrogant enough to dismiss anyone. We dominated the Jets that day, holding them to just a field goal, 164 total yards, and 46 rushing yards. It was an easy day for the defense: we were on the field for just over twenty minutes because the offense possessed the ball at will. I had six tackles against New York, our defense had two sacks, and my former teammate in New England, Curtis Martin, had 29 yards on 15 attempts.

We repeated our defensive excellence the next week in a Buffalo snowstorm, crushing the Bills 35–7. I gained a lot of confidence from a play that led to one of my teammates, James Sanders, scoring a touchdown. I was able to instinctively turn my palms upward and tip a pass by Buffalo quarterback J. P. Losman. The ball fluttered and was picked by James, who returned it for a score. Those are the plays I was used to making. Although I had made similar plays before, that particular one was a satisfying confidence builder.

It's hard to believe, but the defense was on the field for just eighteen minutes in Buffalo. Suddenly we were 8–5, with a Saturday game coming up against a playoff-bound Tampa team. I was proud of what we were accomplishing. Starting with the second half of our Kansas City loss, we had gone ten quarters and given up a total of 17 points.

The number of points allowed did not budge after the next week, when we shut out the Buccaneers, 28–0. Statistically, it was my best game of the season. I had 11 tackles, 2 sacks, a forced fumble, and a pass defensed. It was a tremendous moment for our team as well, and not just because it pushed our record to 9–5. The victory meant that we had won our division. We legitimately had a chance to reach our goal, something that had seemed unlikely just a few weeks earlier in Kansas City. We were well into December, a week away from Christmas, and we were on a streak in which no December opponent had gained as much as 200 total yards.

My in-laws were in New England for Christmas because their hometown, Tucson, was something like 85 degrees. They are Nebraskans at heart, and they believe that part of the Christmas charm is cold weather and snow. For our team, Christmas Day dinner would actually have to take place on Christmas Eve. We were scheduled to play the final *Monday Night Football* game in ABC's history against the Jets on December 26. That meant we would be home on Christmas morning, but we would have to travel to New Jersey on Christmas afternoon. A couple days before Christmas, I asked Tom Brady what his plans were for the day.

"I'm just going to hang out," he said.

"Well, you gotta come over to the house," I told him. "Come over and have dinner and hang out with the kids."

He said he would consider it, which surprised me. I extended the invitation, but I had no idea whether he'd accept or not. I knew that his family was on the West Coast, and that their holiday activities were probably going to take place in the San Francisco area. I wanted to make it clear that he was more than welcome to join us in North Attleboro. He wound up e-mailing me later, saying he was coming over and wondering what the plan for the day was going to be. When he arrived, his hands were not empty. He had gifts for the kids as well as a Monet book for Heidi and me. Before we had dinner, I wanted us to attend a mass at St. Mary's in North Attleboro. I knew there would be a lot of people at church, so we got there an hour early to save a pew. And it was still too late. The church was packed. We stood in the back with dozens of others, and the only time anyone seemed to notice that we played for the Patriots was the portion of mass where you offer peace to your neighbors. At home, everyone seemed to enjoy the dinner conversation and, of course, the food. I was able to talk with Tom in detail about the stroke and some of the challenges I had faced on my way back to the team. It was a good day all around.

The next day the team traveled to New Jersey, knowing that the final two games of the season were for minor playoff positioning. We had five losses, so it was impossible for us to catch either Indianapolis or Denver, the top two teams in the AFC. We knew we were guaranteed a home playoff game, although we had no idea of our seeding or opponent. It would be the first time our Super Bowl run did not begin with a first-round bye. We've won two conference titles on the road, both in Pittsburgh, but when we've won Super Bowls, we've never had to get there by winning three postseason games.

On our flight to Giants Stadium, guys were relaxed. Several players own portable video game players that include a Texas hold-'em game. Everyone puts in a small flat fee and the winner gets the pot. I'm not saying that I win every game, but I have been known to go on a winning streak or two. It's pretty cool.

Once the football game began, we didn't handle the Jets as easily as we had three weeks earlier, but there was no question that we controlled the game. We stopped their running game again, we held them to under 200 total yards again, and—remarkably—the offense had the ball for 43 minutes and 21 seconds. We built a 28–7 lead after three quarters and coasted to a 10-point win, 31–21. There was just one problem all night: I got hurt.

It was a routine punt play. I played the left wing and blocked. My job is first to protect, and as I took off I felt a little pop in my left foot. Three years ago in the AFC Championship Game the same thing happened in the other calf. This time, I went to the ground and waved to the trainers. I knew it was trouble. Almost instantly I whispered, "Man, that's gonna be two weeks." Officially, it was a strained calf, and it was going to lead to some missed games.

I wanted to finish out the regular season because I felt that I was starting to play well. To get knocked out like that was a little discouraging, although it was nice to have my calf talked about. In other words, it was an actual football injury. Now, I'm not trying to compare having a stroke to hurting a calf, but my point to anyone who wanted to listen was always that I could get hurt playing football, no matter what had happened to me in February. In any case, I thought it was kind of funny that I had come full circle. There was a time when all anyone wanted to talk about with me was how crazy I was to think about playing football again. The decision to play was debated, and some hard-core Patriots fans didn't want to see me return. When I hurt my calf, I heard people talking about me as a football player again, and the questions were, "How long is he going to be out?" and "Is anything torn?" I wanted them to talk about my calf. It was fine, and it was a lot better than the alternative.

We had ten wins going into the regular-season finale at Gillette against the Dolphins. I knew I wasn't going to play in that game. The plan was to get myself as prepared as possible for our playoff opponent the following week. If we beat the Dolphins, we were going to be matched up with Pittsburgh at home the next week. If we lost, our first-round opponent would be Jacksonville, a team that finished with more wins (12) than us. I was merely a sideline witness when we lost to the Dolphins, 28–26. We were the fourth seed in the playoffs, and now it was time to get ready for the Jaguars. Not only did I think we'd beat them, I honestly believed we wouldn't lose the rest of the season.

THE SUPER BOWL MENTALITY

think my approach to football in January and February is easy to understand: I want to win, and I want to win more than anyone else has won before. I remember having a conversation with Roman Phifer, one of my former teammates, and we both felt it was important to win so often that no critic or skeptic could ever consider it an accident.

We talked about it after we won our second Super Bowl in Houston, over the Carolina Panthers. Frankly, winning two Super Bowls was not enough. You have to win three in a short span to be considered special—to start talking about dynasties—and that's why Super Bowl XXXIX in Jacksonville will always be my favorite one. It's the game that gave us the privilege to call ourselves great without preface or apology.

As strange as it sounds, you have to do more than win the big postseason games to be a champion. There is an air of complacency that you have to squash, and it's hard to do because you're fighting human nature. Training camp becomes different because you're the Super Bowl champs, and sometimes, honestly, you don't want to work as hard. It's easy to feel that way if you don't have the right attitude, and especially if you've just won your first Super Bowl. Look what's happened to some of the teams that have won and lost Super Bowls: Philadelphia lost to us in Jacksonville and didn't make the playoffs the next season; Carolina lost to us the year before and then missed the playoffs; Tampa Bay beat the Raiders and both franchises haven't been the same since.

Looking at the trend makes me even more proud of what the Patriots have been able to do. We won our first Super Bowl, went 9–7 and didn't make the playoffs the next year, and then won back-to-back championships. That's a credit to the players and the head coach. I'm obviously biased on this subject, but anyone who has ever been part of a championship team can tell you that getting back to that level requires a great deal of mental toughness and talent. I think it also takes superior coaching, but there are also times when the leaders on the team have to be player-coaches as well. A small example of that can be found in the way we handle players who are late to meetings. When I first came into the league, the Patriots played at Foxboro Stadium. It was a facility that was slapped together for $6 million and there was nothing modern about it, including the clocks. They were those old manual ones, and some players turned them back in the meeting rooms to give them more break time. So while one clock upstairs said it was five till, one downstairs said ten or fifteen. You heard all kinds of excuses when some players came in late: "I thought I had plenty of time because the other clock said it was 11:45 . . ."

That doesn't happen now. All the clocks at Gillette are in sync, and the veterans on the team are clock watchers. We actually have fun with it. We come up with a time that will make a guy late for a meeting—let's say it's 9:52—and we fine anyone $100 for every minute they're late after that (it's $200 per minute in the postseason and $300 for the Super Bowl). A lot of times guys will get back to the meeting room a minute or two early just to watch the clock and see if anyone comes in late. It's turned into a sport for us. You wouldn't believe how many times someone sprints into the room with just ten or twenty seconds to spare. I remember when Rodney Harrison first came to our team in 2003. He didn't know about our rule, so when he walked in, Mike Vrabel, Willie McGinest, and I made a ruckus. "That's $100 per minute, Harrison. You're late." We tease him about it now; he was hot over it when he first got here. Now he's one of the leaders of the pack, one of our enforcers.

The cool thing about it is that we're able to take care of it in-house without it blowing up into an issue that requires official paperwork. For example, by NFLPA rules, if you're late for a meeting the cost is $1,700.

I didn't think I was being nostalgic about our previous championship teams when it was time to start the 2005 playoffs. We entered the first round with a nine-game postseason winning streak. You have to be able to do a lot of things, big and small, to put together a streak like that. One of them is knowing how to handle the distractions that playoff games and Super Bowls bring. When we get to the Super Bowl and my friends and family want tickets, they all know that Heidi is the person to talk to. Each player gets a block of tickets and the veterans get the option of purchasing more. As soon as I get them, I hand them over to Heidi and have her take care of them. I'm blessed to have a wife who makes so many sacrifices to ensure that I can focus on the game rather than tickets, hotel rooms, and so on.

By now, most of the players on our team are used to playing in games that generate a lot of attention and hype. I don't think that affects us, either. If anything, it's exciting to have more media members in the locker room than usual and to have so many people talking about the game. Hype never affects the way you prepare. Our preparation is pretty black and white during the week: meetings, weight room, massage days, watching film. It's so structured that it's hard to get distracted.

I was far from distracted before our 2005 playoff opener against the Jaguars. In my mind, the unspoken theme of the entire season could be traced back to Honolulu and Tom Brady's words at the Pro Bowl. He talked about three Super Bowl wins in a row, a historic achievement, and I think his message resonated with a group of players who were eager to be a part of something that would be smiled upon by history. It was going to be an interesting challenge, because while we didn't have all of our best players available, we did have a great postseason résumé. Just remembering the postseason run of the previous year was enough to give us confidence.

In 2004, our first playoff game was against the Colts at Gillette. Peyton Manning was the league MVP with 49 touchdowns and just 10 interceptions. We had knocked off the Colts the year before in the AFC Championship Game, a game in which Ty Law intercepted Manning three times. Law was hurt in 2004, and our cornerbacks were Randall "Blue" Gay, Asante Samuel, and Troy Brown. Brown was exclusively a receiver the first eleven years of his career, but because of injuries in the secondary, he had over 200 snaps as a cornerback. Although we had fourteen regular-season wins and earned a first-round bye, we weren't expected to beat the Colts. Most media people didn't think our secondary could hold up against Manning, Marvin Harrison, Reggie Wayne, and Dallas Clark. To me, the first sign that it was going to be our day was the snow that began to fall shortly before the game. I'll never forget standing in the snow during warm-ups and having a security guard motion to me. "Hey," he said, pointing to the snow, "Bob Kraft must have a pipeline to the Man Upstairs." We loved playing in bad-weather games and we got the impression that the Colts didn't. We also knew that they didn't appreciate our style of play. We wanted to be physical; we wanted to hit them when they had the ball and even hit them when they didn't. We also wanted to hit them when they didn't expect it, which is exactly what happened during a key play I had against Dominic Rhodes.

We had a 6–0 lead midway through the second quarter, but the Colts had driven to our 29. A penalty backed them up 10 yards to our 39, and from there it was obvious that Manning was trying to set up a screen to Rhodes. You can tell many times it's a screen because offensive linemen will allow defenders to penetrate a little too easily. The running back tries to sort through the traffic, get the timing right for the rushers to pass him, and then he tries to slip out. That's what Rhodes did. I had one man to beat, the center, and I was able to simply outrun him and make him miss. So when I got to Rhodes he was just receiving the ball from Manning. It was a different kind of hit because we were practically face mask to face mask. I was able to look at his eyes and could tell that he was a little stunned to see me. The ball was mine as much as it was his, so I wrapped him up and put my left hand between the ball and his shoulder pads. Coaches always talk about the three points of pressure: the fingers, the elbow, and the rib cage. If you're carrying the ball and you allow a defender to attack one of those pressure points, you're in trouble. For Rhodes, he didn't have the ball tucked into his elbow or pressed against his ribs. I felt that I could take it from him. I didn't have a good grip on the ball, but I could feel it slipping out of his hands and into my rib cage. At that point I fell to the ground because I knew I could control it better there. The ball was ours.

We allowed the Colts just 3 points that day, and I was fired up about it. I was still mad about the conference championship game in 2003 against the Colts. That's the year they did a lot of complaining about how we were playing physically 5 yards beyond the line of scrimmage. Well, we were. We believe there are different rules for the playoffs. Things aren't going to be given to you. You have to earn it. The year before, it was 4th-and-10 and they wanted the officials to call holding on Phifer against tight end Marcus Pollard. It's potentially the last play of your season and you're looking to be bailed out by a holding call? It's not going to happen, especially in the playoffs. Our attitude is that we're mentally and physically tougher than the other guys. Smarter and tougher—that's what we pride ourselves on.

We needed every ounce of toughness and intellect the next week in Pittsburgh. We respected their philosophy and we respected a lot of their players (a few who stood out to me were Troy Polamalu, Aaron Smith, Hines Ward, Jerome Bettis, and a couple of special teamers, Sean Morey and Clint Kriewaldt). They had just one loss during the year and their running game was rolling. They had two massive men at running back in Duce Staley and Bettis. I think a lot of people are surprised by Duce when they see him up close; you don't realize what a big man he is. He's got such a wide lower body that tackling him low—which I like to do for the sure tackle—is tough. We also had to acknowledge what they did to us earlier in the season on Halloween. They beat us up pretty bad: physically, points, running all over us, everything. One of the Steelers, linebacker Joey Porter, had a lot to say that day. He kept yelling to us, "You will never be on our level." We had already won two Super Bowls at that point, including one in which we went to Pittsburgh and won the AFC championship in 2001. What level was he talking about exactly? The Steelers and Porter still didn't have a ring at that point.

I was happy that we were able to surprise them a little in the 2004 conference title game, jumping out to a 17–3 lead in the second quarter. The Steelers were in the red zone late in the second quarter, trying to make the score a respectable 17–10 before halftime. Part of our game plan was to take away the deep ball, where quarterback Ben Roethlisberger has excellent accuracy, and cover all the underneath routes closely. We wanted Roethlisberger to come off his first read and consistently go to his second one. We were banking that he wouldn't have the same accuracy on his second read, and he might even be pressured by his internal clock; we wanted him to feel like he had to rush to get rid of everything. Fortunately for us, Rodney was in good position playing man coverage as the Steelers drove before half-time. He stepped in front of an underthrown Roethlisberger pass at the Pittsburgh 13 and returned it 87 yards for a touchdown. With a 24–3 lead, we knew we were going to be headed to Super Bowl XXXIX. The final score was 41–27.

Two weeks later we were in Florida, trying to secure our third title. I looked at the Eagles as a team that relied heavily on the West Coast offense, and I felt that we could disrupt that timing with our overall physicality. I respected them, but I honestly felt that we were the better team and if we played our game we'd be all right.

I do remember being impressed that Terrell Owens was playing in the game when no one thought he'd be able to do it after breaking his leg toward the end of the regular season. Later, in Hawaii, I went up to him before the start of the Pro Bowl and told him that I thought it was great that he played in the game. He was out on the field, with his headphones on, and Donovan McNabb was close by. I told him that doing what he did showed a lot of guts and he should be applauded for it. If he just would have been cool about it during the off-season instead of demanding more money, I think things would have worked out for him in Philadelphia. I don't support anything that Owens did, but I will say that when players do what Owens did in the Super Bowl—insisted on playing even though he was hurt—they almost feel that they are worth more money. It's something that we all feel, and I'm sure it creeps into all of our minds. I know it's happened to me from time to time. The difference, though, is that most players have the ability to come back to earth and say, "It's my job; I'm simply doing what I'm paid to do." Owens wasn't like that.

For us, things obviously worked out when we played the Eagles. We won, 24–21, and one of the remaining mysteries—especially for Eagles fans—is why the team didn't play with more offensive urgency when we had a 10-point lead with less than six minutes left. The clock was running and they were huddling up. I remember looking at that, raising my eyebrows, and turning back to our defensive huddle wondering, "What are they thinking?" They were able to score, but it took them thirteen plays and nearly four minutes to do it. They had one final chance to force a tie or even get a win with forty-six seconds left. Josh Miller landed a sweet punt at the Philadelphia 4, meaning the Eagles were going to have to use some incredible clock management just to get into field goal range.

I thought to myself, "They do have some playmakers on this team. Anything can happen." Instead, McNabb threw a check-down the very first play to Brian Westbrook for a yard, and he was tagged by Phifer. I was shocked: they didn't have any timeouts left and they were accepting a play that kept the clock running. It was amazing. I was elated and stunned at the same time. I knew it was over then, no matter what happened. After an incomplete pass left seventeen seconds on the clock, I decided I was going to rush the quarterback and that there was a great chance I could wind up with a safety. I had Westbrook in man coverage, and I thought I'd be able to blow by him and get the sack. But McNabb threw before I could get to him, and the ball landed in the hands of Rodney.

We had our third championship and not only did I have a bucket of water for Bill Belichick, I had one for Romeo Crennel as well. Romeo hadn't said anything during the week, but all the players knew that this was his last game as our defensive coordinator. He was on his way to Cleveland to become the head coach of the Browns. I was proud of him and so were a lot of the guys. He was a good coach, and we had a lot of love for him. As silly as it sounds, I was happy that I had the chance to give Belichick a Gatorade shower. Our previous two Super Bowls had ended on the last play of the game, so there wasn't time to coordinate the bucket dump. I sprinted as fast as I could off the field, grabbed the bucket that was filled with more ice than water, and drenched Bill and his dad. He never saw it coming. After a few seconds, I grabbed Bill by that funky gray sweatshirt and gave him a hug.

Not long after the Super Bowl, I was faced with the biggest physical and mental challenge of my life. While playing football is not the most important thing in my life, it is what I do for a living. So getting back on the field and back to the postseason had added meaning to me in 2005.

My playoff week in January 2006 didn't get off to the best start. I was rehabbing my injured calf and I probably pushed too hard. Five days before the Jaguars game, I felt that I had reaggravated the injury. It was too bad, because I'm convinced that I aggravated it on my last drill of the day. The trainers want you to push yourself, but they also want you to be honest about how you're feeling. I was pushing myself, but I pushed too much. The game was on Saturday, so I had some time to get the calf to a point where I might be able to participate. I made a lot of progress on the day of the game.

"I think I can go," I said to Bill, even though I hadn't practiced all week.

Bill said he'd activate me and put me in if the team needed me. Monty Beisel, who had gotten all the reps in practice, started the game. While I wanted to play, it turned out that the team got by without me. We controlled Jacksonville's running game, so it quickly turned into a nickel-and-dime defense for us. If I had played, I would have been on the field only when we were in the 3–4 defensive alignment. I thought it was Monty's best game of the year, we did a lot of good things against the run, and Willie McGinest finished the night with 4½ sacks, making him the all-time postseason leader. It was a 7–3 game after two quarters, but we scored two touchdowns in the third on huge plays by Asante Samuel and Ben Watson. We eventually put the game away, 28–3.

I could sense our confidence as well as that of the New England fans. After a great December and 3 points allowed on the first Saturday in January, there was a feeling that we had enough to go into Denver and win a divisional playoff game there. The Broncos-Patriots game in the regular season had been the last Patriots game I watched on TV. It was that day in October when the Patriots released the official statement clearing me to return to football. In the game, the Broncos got a huge lead on us before holding off a comeback and winning, 28–20.

I knew we could beat them, even though the game was at their place. The Denver offense revolves around the running game, which is sort of defined as a one-cut style. The running back takes the ball and runs in unison with the offensive linemen. Each of those linemen has a zone to block. The back makes his read, makes one cut, and then goes downhill. Our 3–4 system is one where the defensive linemen stand their opponents up and allow the linebackers to make plays. But when we play Denver, our defensive linemen have a little more freedom because the players they face are constantly moving; the Broncos are not going to stand there and try to drive it down your throat, because they're not really built for that. I felt that our linemen would have no problem getting upfield, and the linebackers would have to read and react to what the linemen did.

Based on the men we have up front, I always have reason to be confident. One of the players who I feel is vastly underrated is 300-plus-pound defensive end Ty Warren. We're talking about someone who can literally manhandle someone. He is ironically nicknamed "Tiny." He can easily take on someone who is 350 pounds. That commands a lot of respect. And I've seen guys do it a lot of different ways: giving ground, then trying to shed off a block or an arm under/arm over approach. With Tiny, the no-frills physicality and size is right up there with Richard Seymour. It's right up there in his technique and his ability against the run.

As the divisional playoff began in Denver, with 77,000 fans mostly dressed in orange, I felt that the game was going exactly as I expected. Their offense didn't do anything that surprised us: they are who they are, so they tried to establish their running game against us. They gained just 16 yards on their first six running plays. That's not to say that they were going to abandon the run, because they wouldn't do that unless we got up a couple touchdowns on them. But I think they could sense that it wasn't going to be easy moving the ball against us on the ground.

The early indication was that quarterback Jake Plummer would have to make some plays if the Broncos were going to pull the game out.

After a scoreless first quarter and 3–3 game as we approached halftime, I was shocked by a play Plummer made—with some help from number 12, Gregory Steed. Steed is not a Denver receiver; he's a back judge on referee Jeff Triplette's crew. The Broncos had the ball at our 40, and on first down Plummer attempted to hit receiver Ashley Lelie deep along the left sideline. Lelie was being covered well by Asante Samuel, and the receiver even initiated contact with Samuel as they both went for the ball. Most people watching it thought it was a clean football play and an incomplete pass. The side judge was on top of it and didn't reach for his flag. Lelie, unlike most receivers who feel they've been interfered with, didn't say anything to the officials as the ball fell to the ground. But Steed reached for his flag and said it was interference, with the ball spotted at our 1.

I couldn't believe how bad the call was. I'm usually a good cop to the officials while other players are bad-copping them. Sometimes you need a mediator, and I usually fill that role. But I couldn't do it that time. I hadn't told off an official in years, but I went to Steed and said, "You're awful." I said it to him in the huddle, just as he was backing away. He didn't respond. I just felt so bad about that call that I had to let it out. Denver hadn't earned those yards, and it upset me that Steed had given them to the Broncos. We knew how Asante felt because we all felt the same way. Denver scored a touchdown from the 1, and they took a 10–3 lead into halftime.

In the second half, it was as if impostors stole our uniforms and called themselves the Patriots. We had won ten consecutive postseason games because of our preparation, talent, and smart handling of the football. But we fell apart in the second half. Just as there had been a game-turning play at the end of the second quarter, there was one at roughly the same time at the end of the third. We were trailing 10–6 with the ball at the Broncos' 5-yard line. I knew we'd come out of that situation with some kind of points. On third down, Tom looked for Troy Brown in the back of the end zone. Champ Bailey made a play on the ball, intercepted it, and ran it 100 yards to our 1. He didn't score because tight end Ben Watson made a great hustle play, running from the other side of the field to chase Bailey down. He tackled him with such ferocity that Bailey fumbled and the ball appeared to go out of the end zone, which would have resulted in a touchback. Bill challenged the official's call and lost. So instead of us closing the gap to 10–9 or taking a 13–10 lead, Denver scored from the 1 to make it 17–6.

It wasn't going to be our night. We turned the ball over five times, and when you turn it over five times in the playoffs you should lose, home or away. Other than the pass interference call, I don't have too many complaints about how the game was officiated. To me, the story was turning it over; you turn it over, you usually lose. Or said another way: whenever a punter forces a fumble—as Todd Sauerbrun did on Ellis Hobbs—it's not going to be your night. The final score was 27–13, and I didn't take it well. I can't remember the last time I was so hurt after a loss, and that includes our loss to Green Bay in Super Bowl XXXI in New Orleans. I cried after the game, and I felt the loss on multiple levels. First, there was the shock of losing. I kept thinking that if we had won the game, anything could have happened for the AFC Championship Game. I was right: Pittsburgh beat Indianapolis the next day, so the conference title game would have been at Gillette against the Steelers.

I remember Dean Pees coming up to me and congratulating me for all I had done to get back on the field. Eric Mangini, our defensive coordinator, approached me and said, "Helluva comeback, Bru. It was absolutely incredible what you did." I thanked them both as best as I could, but I kept thinking the same thing: It's over. Not just the season, but my career. Right after the game, I thought I was done. I didn't know if I wanted to come back in 2006 because I hadn't thought about it yet.

I'm at the stage of my career where I don't just assume that I'll be back next year. After each season, I think really carefully about how I feel about the next season. I think about my family and how I'm a veteran in the football world, but I'm still a young father. Really, how many years do I have left? Two or three? There are times when I think about playing until TJ is in the second or third grade. A couple years ago, I had a conversation with Larry Izzo and Ted Johnson after one of our walkthroughs. We asked one another, "How many years is enough to play in the league?" Larry and Ted both said ten to twelve. I looked at them—and I think it was my eighth year—and said, "How about nine?"

More than ever, I know that anything can happen in a year. I was hurting after the loss to Denver, and the hurt stayed with me for a long time. I was home watching the playoffs and doing a lot of thinking. I watched the Steelers display a lot of toughness by going into the postseason as a wildcard team and winning three road games on their way to the Super Bowl. You get to the Super Bowl like that and win it, well, you're a deserving champion. As I watched them win and as I thought more about the things we didn't accomplish in 2005, I made up my mind for 2006. Rodney was going to come back from his season-ending injury in 2005, and I wanted the chance to play with him again. I wanted the chance to win another Super Bowl, which would give us four titles in six years, something that the great Pittsburgh teams did in the 1970s. Retire? It just wasn't my time yet. I was determined to return in 2006 and win.

12

ONCE MORE INTO THE BREACH

On the last day of a hotter-than-normal July in Greater Boston, I lay on the Gillette Stadium grass preparing for what I thought would be an ordinary tackling drill. It was the sixth session of 2006 training camp and I was just thankful to be on the field with nothing to worry about but football. At this point, I was more likely to see Dr. Greer socially than at the hospital. There were no issues to monitor as there had been the year before, so now it was simply time to hit somebody.

I was on my back, about ten yards away from running back Heath Evans, who was also lying on his back. At the sound of the whistle, the two players in this particular drill are supposed to simultaneously leap to their feet with the defender finding a way to bring the runner down. It's something I've done many times in nearly a dozen training camps. But on this day, as Evans ran, I tried to tackle him and strip the ball away in the process. As I fell to the ground, I put out my right hand to brace my fall and landed awkwardly on the wrist, but I didn't think anything of it. In fact, I lined up to do the drill again, this time facing Corey Dillon, but Bill Belichick blew the whistle and wanted to move on to something else.

After the morning practice, I noticed that there was a throbbing in my wrist that I hadn't noticed thirty minutes earlier. It was an intense, stabbing pain, one that made me search for trainer Jim Whalen. We both agreed, initially, to wait until after the second practice of the day to get X-rays on the wrist. There wasn't going to be enough time for me to get X-rays and make the next practice. But when ice didn't help and the pain became worse, it was clear that I needed immediate attention.

"Jim, if we have to miss practice, it's all right," I said to him. "We have to figure out this wrist."

It was so tender that as an intern drove me to get X-rays, I told him to avoid the bumps; even the slightest movement would cause the wrist to scream. Eventually, after the swelling went down, I found out the issue: I had broken the scaphoid bone in my wrist. I was going to need surgery and, for the second season in a row, I was going to miss the entire exhibition season. I tried to think of things positively. Hey, you don't need the exhibition season anyway. You'll be back for the season opener. I had surgery on the wrist and tried to focus on the opener against Buffalo. But three weeks later, I was still in pain. It was the first of September, a week and a half before the start of the season, and my wrist was still swollen, red, and sore.

Jim and his staff tried everything. They experimented with several casts, but none of them worked for me. There would be days when Jim would set me up with a cast and then go to the practice field as I did some cardio exercises inside. He wouldn't be outside long because, inevitably, I'd call him back in and ask for something, anything, that would do a better job of stabilizing the thumb and the wrist. What I couldn't do was have a cast on the wrist because the slightest pressure would cause it to throb.

It was obvious that if I was going to play in 2006—and that certainly was the plan—I was going to have to adapt to playing with one arm. I would have to adjust everything I did related to football: the way I bench-pressed, the way I did bicep curls and triceps extensions, the way I approached offensive linemen and used my hands to shed them, and the way I "wrapped" up backs and receivers and tackled them. There wasn't going to be a lot of wrapping up at all. I was going to become a shoulder player, someone who would lean into opponents and try to knock them down that way or try to hold them with my left arm and wait for my teammates to come along and help me out.

While it was clear that my personal challenge for the season would be performing at a high level with an injured wrist, the team—and specifically the offense—would be challenged to get by without receiver Deion Branch. Branch was the MVP of Super Bowl XXXIX and, statistically, was our best receiver. He was in the final year of his contract and was holding out of training camp until he got a new and much more lucrative deal.

I loosely paid attention to the early days of Deion's holdout. I've seen lots of guys either leave camp or hold out, only to return as if nothing happened. One of my former teammates, Ted Johnson, left the team for a couple days in 2002 and then returned. Ty Law called Belichick a liar after 2003 and said he'd pay Belichick and the Patriots to release him; he came back the next season and was a member of our third Super Bowl team (he got hurt in the seventh game of the 2004 season and was out the rest of the year). Richard Seymour held out in 2005, saying he wanted a contract that would pay him fairly. The team ultimately agreed with Big Sey and gave him a new deal. In all those cases, the disputes were resolved without a trade or a release. I thought the same thing would happen with Deion.

I began to think differently in late August, when the Patriots gave Deion permission to work out a contract with other teams. When that happened, I shouldn't have been shocked—although I was—when Tom Brady relayed some news to me as we talked in the weight room.

"Did you hear about Deion?" Tom said. "We traded him to Seattle."

It was surprising news to all of us, but it was especially tough on the offensive players. They had lost one of the guys who helped them succeed as a unit, and there was probably a little resentment there because they had also expected things to be worked out.

If we were going to win a championship in 2006, we were going to have to do it without some key contributors from the past. Willie McGinest signed with the Browns, David Givens signed with the Titans, Adam Vinatieri, the man whose right foot ended two Super Bowls for us, signed with the Colts, and Deion was a Seattle Seahawk.

Fortunately, in the middle of training camp, we were able to make an important acquisition, someone who would help us physically and spiritually. We all thought Junior Seau, a line-backer headed to the Hall of Fame, had retired in mid-August. That's exactly what he said in a memorable press conference in which he announced that he wasn't retiring but "graduating" to the next phase of his life. The graduation brought him to us less than a week later.

I was excited to have Junior on our team. He has a great reputation in the league, but I was even more amazed when I got to witness how he is every day. From the moment he arrived in our locker room, it was as if he had been there for years. He walked in calling everybody "Buddy," and quickly made himself comfortable with all the stadium facilities. He's a tremendous worker. There were times I'd come in early to watch film and he'd already be there. If he wasn't watching film, he'd be working out or sitting in a hot or cold tub. I could tell that he was smart and conscientious, a guy with a good attitude who was fun to be around. I was looking forward to being on the field with him.

That moment finally came on September 17 in the Meadow-lands against the Jets. I was wearing a long cast that covered my thumb and extended all the way to my elbow. I felt that I could find a way to help the team, despite the clunky cast. There were a couple plays when my assignment was to cover the running back, and Jets quarterback Chad Pennington called a quick option route to the sideline. I was able to step in front of the back and get two hands on the ball, but I was never able to have enough flexibility to control the ball and intercept it. A few times I'd look down at my cast and practically have a conversation with it. *If you weren't here, it would be a lot easier for me to play.* But this was going to be the story the entire season, so I had better get used to it.

We were able to jump on the Jets very quickly. They were coached by Eric Mangini, our former defensive coordinator, so we were very familiar with their mentality and scheme. We had a 17–0 lead at halftime and went up 24–0 in the third quarter. The game looked like it was on its way to being a rout, but the Jets made it interesting with two huge plays in the third quarter. On one, a receiver named Jerricho Cotchery caught a pass and appeared to be hit hard by cornerback Chad Scott. But Cotchery never hit the ground—he actually landed on top of safety Eugene Wilson—and was able to jump up and run to the end zone for a 71-yard scoring play. Later in the quarter, New York receiver Laveranues Coles caught a 46-yard touchdown pass, a play in which he did some spectacular running after the catch.

A blowout suddenly became interesting at 24–14. And then it became a real game in the fourth quarter when Mike Nugent hit a field goal to make it 24–17. Our offense took over the game then. We had the ball for more than half the quarter, putting the Jets in a position where they had to drive 91 yards with about a minute to play and no time-outs. The Jets were able to move the ball from their 9 to their 45, but there were only fifteen seconds remaining. It was time for them to take some shots down the field. Pennington dropped back and lofted a pass that was headed for either of our safeties, Eugene Wilson or Rodney Harrison. As the ball was in the air, I remember telling myself to just react to the play that Eugene or Rodney was certain to make. They looked like they were both going to have a play on it, which meant there was a good chance I could retrieve it on a deflection.

Sure enough, Rodney was there for the easy interception, but Eugene came in and broke up the pass. The ball was floating through the air and it landed softly enough that I could control it, bulky cast and all. It was funny. Rodney was so mad that he forgot to congratulate me on the pick. He was in Eugene's face saying, "What are you doing?" It wasn't the best interception of my career in terms of the things I did to get it, but it was still significant.

I remember having a long conversation with Dr. Greer about what it took for me to intercept a football. He asked me to explain it to him, step by step, so he could get a neurological sense of what I was doing as I went for the ball. So I talked to him about recognizing the flight of the ball, getting my hands placed properly so I could squeeze it, and then recognizing where I am on the field so I can possibly turn and run with it. He listened to it all and said, "I'm confident in telling you that you're back to normal physically. But one thing I can't tell you—one thing I don't know—is if you'll be the same player again."

As usual, he would make jokes when he saw me. During the last half of the 2005 season, he would tease me about stats. "Where are the sacks? Where are the forced fumbles? Where are the interceptions?" I gave him sacks and forced fumbles, but he was staying on me about the interceptions. So when I finally got one in 2006, on that heave from Pennington, I held on to the ball and sent it to Dr. Greer. I wrote, "To Dr. Greer . . . Come-back complete." He was surprised when the football arrived at his office. "That ball said 'Jets' on it," he said. "Is that the real ball from the game?"

Only two games into the season, I was feeling good about our team and our defense. Coach Pees had replaced Eric as defensive coordinator, and he was putting his own stamp on the defense. He was able to run a variety of defenses from a "Cover 4" base, which is when the two safeties are deep and shaded toward the number two receiver. It was also a tremendous help to have Junior on the field in our 3–4 defense. With him playing inside linebacker with me, that allowed us to play Mike Vrabel at his best position, which is outside linebacker. I always tell Mike that if we allowed him to play outside all year and rush the passer, he'd be in the Pro Bowl. He's just a great player with a knack for getting to the quarterback. He's also so versatile that we often don't leave him at one position. He has played inside, he's played the Will, or weak-side, linebacker position, and he's been the Money, which is what we call the linebacker who covers tight ends in our sub packages.

We began the year by winning six of our first seven games. On average, our defense was allowing fewer than 14 points per game. With a 6–1 record in early November, we had back-to-back games against the Colts and the Jets. With the number of big games that we've played against the Colts in the last few seasons, sometimes it seems like we're in the same division. They were returning to Gillette at roughly the same time they had in 2005, when they ran away from us on *Monday Night Football* and scored 40 points. One year later, the game was a lot more competitive, although it was extremely sloppy for us. We turned the ball over five times and the Colts walked away with their second consecutive win over us, 27–20. We also left the game knowing that we'd be without Rodney Harrison for several weeks. He made a tackle and fractured his scapula, literally a tough break for the rock of our secondary. He had worked so hard to get back on the field after his knee problems, and now he was most likely going to be out a month and a half.

The Jets were in Foxboro the next week, playing against us on our hopelessly muddy field. It was hard for either team to get footing on the uneven and dangerous surface, but the Jets were still able to move us off the ball when they needed to. It was raining that day, which made the sledding even tougher. The Jets were able to leave our stadium with a smart and gritty 17–14 win. There were a few times during the game when the Jets made what I would call "Patriots plays." They were able to do things to us that we've done to other teams. One play in the third quarter stands out to me. It was 4th-and-5, and the Jets had the ball at our 33. They appeared to be set to go for the first down because Pennington and the offense stayed on the field. But instead of going for it, Pennington got the ball and punted it to our 4. It was going to be a game of field position, so it was the right call at the right time. It was one of the few times that I said to myself, "Nice job, Eric."

The biggest change for our team following the loss to the Jets was easy for most people to see. Overhead blimp shots of Gillette on TV showed a muddy brown strip with flecks of green down the middle. Local and national fans saw a modern stadium that contained brown grass or brown spots where the grass used to be. The players were thrilled when the league allowed Mr. Kraft to change the surface to field turf during the season.

Our first game with the new turf came on a Sunday night against the Chicago Bears. The Bears were establishing themselves as the best team in the NFC, and they were going to provide a good challenge for us. I thought we played one of our sloppier games of the year, turning the ball over five times as we won, 17–13. As bad as it is to turn the ball over five times, that wasn't even the worst part of the night. In the second quarter, Junior went to tackle Chicago running back Cedric Benson. Junior's right arm got caught and it was obvious to anyone watching that he broke it. His season was over after eleven games and some real inspired play at inside linebacker. It was a pleasure to have him as a teammate. I just wish I could have played with him longer.

Without Junior, Mike Vrabel had to move again to inside linebacker while Tully Banta-Cain played outside. Our record was 8–3 and we were heading into December, the preface to playoff season. With three losses, all in the conference, it was going to be tough for us to secure one of the top two seeds in the playoffs. The Chargers were being called the best team in all of football, the Ravens weren't far behind, and the Colts had knocked us off a few weeks earlier. So we had a lot of teams to pass in terms of playoff seeding. What we focused on, as usual, was methodically handling things in our own games. There were times, though, when it was hard to be methodical—such as our final game of the regular season in Nashville.

Our record in December was 3–1 as we headed to Tennessee for our New Year's Eve game there. Overall our record was 11–4, and we still had a chance to be the third seed in the playoffs. The Titans were 8–7 and had a slim chance of making the postseason. I could tell early that it was going to be an extremely physical game. The Titans had Kevin Mawae at center, and we all knew what kind of player he was from his time with the Jets. I respect him as a player, but he's a guy who will use all of the tricks. He'll grab your arm. He'll push you in the back after a play is done. He'll do whatever he can to set an aggressive tone for the rest of the offensive line.

Mawae must be a great leader, because on New Year's Eve there was an entire line of guys trying to play like him. On one play I was holding up one of their backs, Travis Henry, waiting for a teammate to arrive and attempt to strip the ball from him. As the whistle was blowing and Henry started to fall to the ground, Mawae came in and hit me in the side. And that's what started an afternoon of cheap shots, threats, and near-anarchy on the field.

I got up and started pushing some players, and players from both teams started pushing one another. The curses were flowing freely. Even the officials became aggressive, trying to send the message to us all that they weren't going to tolerate a game that was quickly becoming dirty. I thought the dirtiest moment of all came in the second quarter, when a Titans receiver named Bobby Wade—who went to my alma mater, the University of Arizona—tried to block Rodney Harrison. Rodney was playing in his second game after returning from the shoulder injury he had against the Colts in early November. Obviously, you can always get hurt playing football. But what's disappointing is when you know an injury could have been avoided, when you know that someone else's poor judgment prevents you from being on the field.

That's what happened when Bobby Wade unnecessarily went to block Rodney in his knees. The receiver looked Rodney in the eyes and readied himself as if he were going to take him on up high. Then, at the last second, he went low. That's dirty. That's cheap. Look, we've all been cut-blocked before. When it's a clean cut, you can prepare for it. You can tell by the way the lineman drops his head and then goes low. In that case, you can put your hands on him, play off the block, or, sometimes, there's nothing you can do and you just go down. But you don't do it the way Wade did. The officials said the block was legal and clean, but I didn't think so at the time and I still don't.

When Rodney was hit low, he turned in the air and then hit the ground. He pounded the grass, and when I went near him I could hear him saying, "Bobby, why? Why did you do that, Bobby?" I knew all the effort Rodney had put in the past two years, just to be on the field. I also had an idea that this hit might keep him out of some important playoff games. I leaned close to him.

"Did he hit you low?" I asked.

He nodded.

I didn't need to hear anything else. I headed toward the Tennessee sideline and Bobby Wade. He was standing behind their head coach, Jeff Fisher. I unloaded several obscenities on him, lashing out in a way that I had never done before on a football field. "You're a jerk," I said. "I'm going to kill you."

I remember Fisher looking at me like I was crazy, and a few players stepped in to hold me back. One of the players was their quarterback, Vince Young, who's actually a very nice kid. Some of my teammates, too, held me as I tried to snatch Bobby Wade from the Titans sideline. I was yelling, determined to get him, when I heard a voice.

"Tedy, this is Ed. You need to calm down."

It was Ed Hochuli, the game's referee. Hearing his voice kind of snapped me out of my tirade. But then I walked back over and said some more. After the game resumed, there were a couple of plays toward the Tennessee sideline that put me in earshot of Wade.

"You ain't no Wildcat, Tedy," he said. "You ain't no Wildcat."

I thought it was strange that he thought my logic would work that way: that somehow, because he happened to attend the University of Arizona, I would excuse some dirty play that he did. Don't get me wrong, I spent five years at Arizona and have high loyalties to the place. But that's not what it's about anymore. There were some jerks at Arizona when I went there, too, and he's one of those jerks who doesn't understand what it's about. Sure, we went to the same college, but that was my brother he cut down. He does something like that and we're supposed to have a connection because we went to the same school? Please.

We wound up winning the Tennessee game easily, 40–23. As we boarded the plane for Providence, we still had no idea who we'd meet in the playoffs. When the Broncos lost at home to San Francisco in overtime, the field was set. For the third time in the season, we were going to be facing our divisional rival, the New York Jets. There was a buzz on the plane when word got around. We knew it was going to be a week of drama, starting with Belichick versus Mangini. There's so much history between the franchises and the players that communicating with buddies during the week was a given.

I think our loss to the Jets in November really legitimized them as a team that was for real. Had we beaten them that day in Foxboro, maybe we would have subconsciously thought, "Aw, it's the Jets. We'll spank them around." We went into the game with the mentality that it was going to be tough for us to win. The one player who could present a lot of problems for us was Coles. Really, both Coles and Cotchery had made big plays against us in the first two games.

In the wildcard playoff game at Gillette, Cotchery was there again in the second quarter. We led 7–3 at the time, but Pennington was able to find a hole in the Cover 2 defense we were playing. He passed to Cotchery, who was able to get by everyone for a 77-yard scoring play. The Jets led 10–7, their last lead of the day. We were up 17–10 at halftime, when CBS conducted an interview that none of us saw live but we would all find interesting later. The CBS panelists spoke with San Diego linebacker Shawne Merriman and asked his thoughts on the second half of our game with the Jets. He said he believed the Jets were going to make more plays and pull it out. He was wrong. The game was close until the fourth quarter, when touchdowns on offense and defense—by Kevin Faulk and Asante Samuel—pushed us to a 37–16 win.

The victory meant that we were going to play the Chargers, the number one seed in the AFC, in San Diego. I had heard about Merriman's comments during the interview, and that just set the tone for the whole week. I don't know how many of his teammates felt the same way he did, but it seemed to me there was a general attitude that we were just an opponent that probably shouldn't be there.

I looked at their offense on film, and there were plenty of impressive things there. I felt that LaDainian Tomlinson was a special player, the type of player you might see once or twice every ten years. He was someone who could score from anywhere on the field, and it appeared that he was unstoppable in open space. I liked how physical their offensive line was, and it was clear they had a tight end who could create some unfavorable matchups for us. Their quarterback, Philip Rivers, was solid. He was selected to play in the Pro Bowl over Tom Brady, a fact I still find preposterous. I just don't see how anyone could look at the quarterbacks and say that Rivers had the better season or was the better quarterback. I didn't look at Rivers the same way I looked at Peyton Manning, although Rivers was talking a good game early in the divisional playoff. He would pick up a first down on a quarterback sneak and then get up yelling in our faces, "First down!" He was one of the biggest talkers all day. He paused briefly when Mike Vrabel came up with a comeback designed to silence him.

"You know what? You will never be Drew Brees," he said, mentioning the quarterback that Rivers sat behind for two years. "You know it," Vrabel said, pointing to Rivers. Then he pointed to the San Diego huddle. "And they know it, too."

Mike's comment was humbling, but it wasn't enough to end the day's talking. When San Diego went up 14–3 in the second quarter and 21–13 in the fourth, you could sense just how inexperienced they were with playoff football. It never seemed to occur to them that this day could be the last of their 2006 season. They were a little too comfortable and casual, considering the game situation. Early in the game a couple of their players would brag, "We're going to be here all day." Amazed, I would say, "And where do you think we're going to be? Is the concept of playing for four quarters something new? Do you think we flew all the way out here just to stop playing in the third quarter?"

They didn't know how tough the game was going to be, even when they went up 14–3 and 21–13. I just felt that they thought we were going to fold. No play better summarized our attitude—and theirs—than the one with six and a half minutes left in the game. We had fought all day and were down by 8 points. We had the ball and were driving toward San Diego's end of the field when Chargers safety Marlon McCree intercepted a Tom Brady pass on 4th-and-5. I watched from the sideline and began to put my helmet on, thinking, "Gotta play defense. Gotta get a stop."

But the beauty of our team is that there were a lot of players having the same thought as me. One of them was, technically, an offensive player named Troy Brown. Troy has played his entire career with the Patriots, as wide receiver (his natural position) as well as defensive back and even emergency quarterback in an exhibition game. He has returned kicks and punts, and been part of both coverage units on special teams. He is an all-purpose player who has been a part of three teams that have won Super Bowls and even one that lost it. He was on the field when McCree intercepted that pass at the Chargers' 31, and instead of pouting and assigning blame for the turnover, his thought quickly became, "Gotta play defense. Gotta get a stop."

As McCree ran with the ball and tried to pick up additional yardage, Troy became a ball-hawking defensive back. We are always coached to block the intended receiver when there is an interception, but Troy was unblocked and had a clear path to McCree. He got behind him, tackled him, and separated the ball from the defensive back's body. It was an awesome, season-saving play. As the ball came loose, one of our receivers, Reche Caldwell, fell on it. We were still alive.

I think that play is a snapshot of the playoffs. Things can change suddenly, and you play entire games with that sense of finality. In my opinion, if you don't understand that, you miss the whole point of what the playoffs are. One play and your season can be over and, suddenly, you have no more days of practice and no opponent to prepare for. So now, with new life, we had them thinking a little. We were the road team, down one score against the number one team in the NFL. We finally had them in the position, for the first time all day, of thinking that they could possibly lose this game. And that's the message you want to send, because once you do, the noose starts to tighten a little bit more and the pressure starts to grow.

I didn't hear any more joking from the San Diego players after that. When Tom and the offense got the ball back, they didn't run again. They covered the remaining 32 yards in five plays, ending with a short touchdown to Caldwell. Kevin Faulk ran in the 2-point conversion, and the game was tied with four and a half minutes to play. It was there for either team to win, and we felt that we could take it.

Our defense forced the Chargers to quickly punt when they got the ball, which gave our offense yet another chance to score in regulation. The big play of the drive was a 49-yard pass from Brady to Caldwell, which set up a winning field goal by Stephen Gostkowski.

Shortly after the game was over, I walked into the locker room yelling to no one in particular, "Have a nice time in Hawaii. You can keep your Pro Bowls, and keep your MVPs. We win. That's what we do." I was just letting it out after a game where I felt the opposing team had disrespected us. Besides, the last time we had played in San Diego, in 2002, my family received the worst treatment they've ever had at any stadium in the league. My wife and brother literally felt threatened by the San Diego fans because they were so raucous and rude during the game. It was satisfying to knock off a team that thought it was going to the Super Bowl, and it felt good to do it in front of fans who were thinking the same thing.

So now it was on to something that we had seen before, for the third time in the twenty-first century: Patriots versus Colts in the playoffs. The previous two games had been played in the comfort of New England, with either rain or snow on our previously mangled turf. But this game was going to be played inside, on their carpet, in front of their fans.

The atmosphere in Indianapolis was manic as we took the field. I've heard a lot of comments before games, ranging from the fan in Buffalo who said he wanted me to die to fans in San Diego taunting that I couldn't cover Tomlinson or Antonio Gates. In Indianapolis, I went out to the field to warm up and an older woman shouted, "Tedy, have you taken your nitro? For your heart?" And she tapped her chest.

I shook my head. This was a crowd willing to do anything to give their team an advantage over us, the team that had twice stopped them from where they were trying to go. It looked like it was going to be more of the same in the second quarter when Asante jumped a Marvin Harrison route, intercepted the pass from Manning, and returned it 39 yards for a touchdown. It was 21–3 then, and all I could think was, "We need more."

I knew the Colts were good at making adjustments, and when they scored 3 points just before the half to make it 21–6, I knew the first drive of the second half was going to be a good predictor of what might happen the rest of the way. If we could continue to get pressure on Manning and give the ball to our offense for another score, then maybe I might feel better. But from my experience, you never have a game in the bag at half-time. Never. If we were leading 21–6 late in the fourth quarter, I might think that way.

In the second half, the adjustments were made, and what followed was the best half of football I've ever seen Peyton Manning play. He decided to take advantage of the middle of the field, hitting backs and tight ends. Some of his throws were so precise that I found myself muttering, "Are you kidding me with that?" The throws were right on and so were the routes. It was an overall display of patience and self-control on the part of the Colts, because although many of their plays are designed to go far down the field, they played knowing that there is no such thing as an 18-point play. They took their time and their vastly underrated offensive line wore us down. Their first drive of the third quarter ate up nearly seven minutes and ended with a touchdown that made the score 21–13. They quickly tied it at 21 in the third quarter, and suddenly everyone got the competitive game that was expected.

In the middle of the game, I think it hit me how great the contest was turning out to be. I didn't mind the thought; I just wanted to be sure that we found a way to remember it as a great game that we happened to win. We would go up a touchdown, and the Colts would come back with a touchdown of their own. We would have a field goal, and they'd come back with a field goal of their own. Finally, with us leading 34–31, the Colts had a 3rd-and-2 from our 3-yard line with about a minute to play.

At one point, I looked at Colts left tackle Tarik Glenn and he looked at me. "This is what it's all about," I said. "It's either us or you."

"You're right, man," he said.

He held out his fist and I tapped it with mine. We went back to work, both trying to execute our plans. The Colts had many options to run from the 3. They could keep the ball on the ground, knowing that if we stopped them they could easily kick a tying field goal. They could also throw the ball and go for the lead. We had to be prepared for everything on defense, so we settled on one that overloaded the left side of the line of scrimmage. I moved Vince Wilfork to the left, and I was up on a guard, trying to build a wall for the running game. Colts running back Joseph Addai found a cutback lane and things were just open. Bang. They were up 38–34, with fifty-four seconds to play.

I still believed in us. We had Tom Brady with the ball and two timeouts. I didn't believe it was close to being over, even though we had to go the length of the field and get a touchdown. The offense was able to run four plays, the last of which resulted in an interception. The game was over.

I went up to a few of their guys and offered congratulations. I found Peyton and said, "Congratulations. You were great, and you earned it." I knew we had lost to the better team that day, but I also felt that we squandered an opportunity to add to our legacy. If we had gone to the Super Bowl, we would have been one step closer to being in a historical category that has very few names.

There are nights when I still think about it, when I can't get to sleep because I'm thinking about what could have been. It's tough, but it also added motivation for the 2007 season. I couldn't wait to strengthen my wrist and get going on the off-season program. I was looking forward to playing that season with two hands. I was able to lead our team in tackles in 2006, even though I felt like I did it with one arm and one hand. I thought I could be better in 2007.

Physically, I feel great. If you had asked me in 2005 how often I think about my stroke and my heart, I would have answered, "All the time." But time has healed a lot of my emotional and physical issues. There is no stigma about having a stroke. I've educated myself so I know that there are many faces of stroke, some young and some old. It was something that wasn't comprehensible to me before, and it took me a while to get over that. I'm over it now.

A lot of things have changed since the first day I met Dr. Greer and he put his hand on my shoulder, telling me that I'd had a stroke. For one, the longtime fan of the Pittsburgh Steelers has been converted to a Patriots fan. Another change is that he doesn't need to see me as often as he did in the months after the stroke. He wants me to check in with him twice a year for a general checkup. Other than that, maybe Heidi and I will meet Dr. Greer and his wife, Stephanie, out for dinner, as we did earlier this year. He's a friend, a friend who helped make it possible for me to make two statements: I'm proud to be a football player, and I'm proud to be a stroke survivor.

APPENDIX

American Stroke Association and Tedy's Team

American Stroke Association

The American Stroke Association, a division of the American Heart Association, is solely focused on reducing disability and death from stroke through research, education, fund-raising, and advocacy. The American Heart Association spends more money on heart and stroke research and programs than any other organization except the federal government.

Stroke is a medical emergency. Know these warning signs of stroke and teach them to others. Every second counts:

- Sudden numbness or weakness of the face, arm, or leg, especially on one side of the body
- Sudden confusion, trouble speaking or understanding
- Sudden trouble seeing in one or both eyes
- Sudden trouble walking, dizziness, loss of balance or coordination
- Sudden severe headache with no known cause

Call 9-1-1 immediately if you experience symptoms!
Time lost is brain lost!

Tedy's Team

Led by New England Patriot Tedy Bruschi, Tedy's Team is in its second year of training athletes to complete either the Boston Marathon or the Falmouth Road Race. In furthering the American Stroke Association's mission of reducing disability and death from stroke, Tedy's Team strives to increase recognition and awareness of stroke risk factors and warning signs, and encourage rapid response once the onset of symptoms is recognized.

Team members raise funds to honor a "Stroke Hero," someone in their lives who has been touched by stroke. While participants may have their own personal stroke hero, Tedy also steps forward as an additional stroke hero for each participant. Whether someone runs in support of Tedy or their own stroke hero, the important thing is that they have joined the fight against stroke and are dedicated to do all they can to help the cause.

To support Tedy's Team by making a contribution to the American Stroke Association, or to learn how you can join Tedy's Team, please visit www.strokeassociation.org/tedysteam or www.runtoendstroke.org.